T 7-SECRETS OF CELIBACY

The Single Christian's Guide

On How to Wait on a Mate

Margaret S. Layton

Bryant,
God has a perfect plan,
for you. NO matter what!
Jeremiah 29:11

God Bless
Pearl

The 7-Secrets of Celibacy: The Single Christian's Guide on How to Wait on a Mate, by Margaret S. Layton
Published by Black Pearl Publishing, LLC
Saginaw, MI 48601
www.MargaretSLayton.com

All Scripture References are from the King James Version of the bible unless otherwise noted

The Lord gave The Word: great was the company of those that published it ~ Psalms 68:11

Cover Design: TagDesigns
Front/Back Cover Photo: Ashley J. Beard Photography
Editors: Elaine Allen Karls and Dr. Rose M. Beane

Library of Congress Control Number:
ISBN: 978-0-9836324-1-2
Printed in USA

"What you see,

Write in a book

And send it to the seven churches…"

Revelation 1:11

Contents

Part III

Acknowledgements

There are so many people who have played major roles in my life—too many to name--- but I'd like to give special thanks to:

- My Daddy God. Thank you so much for loving me, not giving up on me, and for protecting me, even when I did not want your protection or know that I needed it. I appreciate you so much. Your love is extravagant and limitless. May I always have a hunger and thirst to do things Your way.

- My daughter Jai who has grown to be a beautiful young lady. It is my love for you Jai that motivated me to change and become whole. May the experiences that I had to encounter to become free never encompass your life or the lives of your children or their children. May the curse of promiscuity be forever cursed at its roots and not harm you, and our future generations, in Jesus' name.

- Delores and Ricky Johnson, my Mom and father for being such great parents and a wonderful example of what it means to ride through the waves of life with God's grace and joy.
- Elaine and Leonard Sherley, my Father and Mother for always loving me and being there for me
- Jessie (Bim) and Wendy McDaniel, my third set of parents who have always treated me like your own (Literally). Bim thanks for causing me to be street smart. The bible calls this wisdom. It is because of your sharp eye to recognize things and people for what and who they really are that I can spot a fake and know the real deal a mile away. I love you and Wendy both dearly.

- My maternal grandparents Luewana and the late Arthur Lee Layton, Sr. thanks for the safe haven that you provided for the entire village (anyone who came into your lives).
- My paternal grandparents, the late Margaret Ree and James Earl Sherley, thanks for being a constant image of wisdom and style in my life.

- Leonard (LL), Brian, Stephanie, and Constance for being the best siblings! I thank God for each of you being your own unique selves and loving me just the way that I am. I love and appreciate you all.

- My Aunts: Christine, Geraldine, Alicia, Shirell, Sherry, Nina, Gwen, and the Late Tracy Stanley. Thanks for being such women of strength and power. Thanks for always encouraging me to reach for God's best. A special thanks to my Naomi, my Tee-Tee Rell. Thanks for leading me to Christ and mentoring me into a movement! My uncles Arthur Jr., Clifford, Ronnie, Robert Sr., Darnell, and Richard. I love you all beyond words.

- My family, the Layton's and the Sherley's for always being there no matter what. A special thank you to my "go-to's" whenever I had a technical question, Larry Layton, Jimmy and Caneesha Medlock and Chaerra Layton! I love and appreciate ALL of my cousins! Christine M. Layton II (Thin Lizzle), Thanks for being there for Jai. April Wicker thanks for my daily "GM" texts! I need them.

- Dr. Ron and Lady Georgette Frierson (who were also pastoral editors. You made sure that my work was scripturally sound). There is none like you. Thank you for seeing pass my past and into my future. Thanks for the many years that you have tirelessly sowed The Word into my heart. Thanks for never giving up on me. Thanks for believing in me and helping me to live in the Philippians 4:19 and Ephesians 3:20 blessing! I love you two to life!

- The entire New Covenant Christian Center Family (Covenites). You are the best church family! Thanks for being, "The church that loves like no other!"

- My God Children E'shon, Laila, Monyea, and LaKennadi. God Mommy loves you. I am ALWAYS praying for you, and I expect God's best from and for you.

- Team Write-Nite for showing up and sharing your dreams and visions of becoming published authors with me. A special shout out to Michelle Reeves (who filled in as peer editor for this project). Your years of writing plays, skits, and leading our ministries MOTA (Ministry of The Arts) Department, along with our longtime friendship of over 20 years, made you the perfect candidate for this assignment. You know my heart, but more importantly you know the heart of God. Thanks for volunteering your time and eagles eye). Minister Sandra Robinson, Onita Coleman, Darnell Barefield, Carmen Hamilton, LaTova Watson, Vicki Harris, Cynthia Taylor, Jessica Patman, Sylvia Brantley, Austin Reeves, Jacquetta and Derrick Dantzler, Author Devonna Carethers and any others who have taken part of Write-Nite in any way. I appreciate you all.

- To Elaine Allen-Karls (who played the role of professional editor). Your profession as an English professor has brought so much wisdom and insight to the direction of this project. Thanks for volunteering your time. Thanks for all of the Barnes and Noble meetings, dinner, prayers, hot chocolate/tea at your house to brainstorm and sort through the clutter in my brain. Your assistance always helps me to get to the content of any project that I may be working on. Thanks for your passion for people, writing, and God. You are THE BEST! Ken thanks for sharing Elaine with me. I love you both!

- Dr. Rose Margaret Beane! Thank you! Thank you! Thank you! For seeing past the subject matter and making sure things were grammatically correct. Words can't express my gratitude for your expertise and encouragement during this project.

- To my LANDS. Some have RODS (Ride Or Dies); I have LANDS (Live And Not Dies): Marcia "Michelle" Reeves, Cherina Johnson, Jacqueline 'Jackie' Jones, RuShawnda McCall, Cynthia Taylor, Dorothea Bandy, Sylvia Brantley, Lawanda Freeman, Minister Sandra Robinson, Dr. Rose M. Beane. Thanks for all of your friendship, love and support.

- To my Face Book family for helping to draw this book out of me through your prayers, encouragement, and questions.

- To anyone that I may have forgotten, thank you. I love you all.

Foreword

What can I say? This is a masterpiece that portrays a victorious single lifestyle. With all the realness that will attract all singles who genuinely want to get it right, live right, while enjoying the process.

In this much needed book, "The Pearl," as I call her is frank and honest in revealing her life on the pages of this great work. This collection of Godly wisdom and insight is a testament to the struggles that all singles must endure to live a life pleasing to God. **"The 7-Secrets of Celibacy: The Single Christian's Guide on How to Wait on a Mate,"** will change the lives of those who are seriously pursuing success in a life of being saved and single.

I have been taught that when truth is embraced change must take place and if you have a passion for change, that change will always be good. I am very proud and honored to write the foreword for this very special book. It is my hope and prayer that you enjoy reading it just as much as I have.

Dr. Ron Frierson
Pastor and Founder of
New Covenant Christian Center Church

We often go through trials, tests, and tribulations that are almost unbearable, while we continue to be faithful to the Lord. However, we must recognize that all that we have belongs to God and we are merely stewards, this includes our bodies. The Bible says, "Your body is the temple of the Holy Spirit" (I Corinthians 1:9) and "every one of you should know how to possess his vessel" (I Corinthians 6:19).

In her book, **"The 7-Secrets of Celibacy: The Single Christians Guide on How to Wait on a Mate"** Miss Layton, also known as Pearl is having a much needed sex talk with single believers everywhere. What has been a private struggle for so many is being brought to the light. If you are a single Christian, it's your time to be set free; to overcome the fleshly desire to have sex outside of the marriage covenant, once and for all.

Pearl also shares her personal journey as a single Christian woman and how she has managed to live celibate for over 17 years in a very candid yet tasteful way. Through these extraordinary truths she shares with her reader what it really means to overcome the flesh and live sexually pure, as you wait on God for a mate.

I have personally witnessed this young woman over the years as she has allowed the light of God's Word to shine through her. What a wonderful example she has been of the contemporary proof that it can be done.

As the author takes you through this journey by using the principles found in God's Word, get ready to laugh and also be challenged as you take the spiritual journey which will lead to success, rewards, and love. Blessings!

Dr. Georgette Frierson
First Lady, Minister, and Teacher of
New Covenant Christian Center Church

Introduction:

Let's Talk About Sex
(*In the Church*)

I n a promiscuously crazed world where, *"everybody's doing it,"* one could only imagine why someone would even talk about, or practice, no less write a book on the subject of celibacy. After reluctantly sharing my 17 year victory (at the time) over sexual sin in the Facebook (FB) post shown on Table 1, I was overwhelmed and humbled by the support, questions, and overall buzz that the topic created. People that I barely knew congratulated me on the feat. Those who still struggle with sexual sin had bold questions about what is considered sexual sin. Single and married people alike told me what a good example I am to their children.

The reason for my hesitation to post such an intimate subject to be seen by the world was that I did not want to appear to be a Miss Goodie-Two-Shoes. In addition, Social media is a place where let's face it, abstinence isn't a very popular topic. I cautiously agreed with God to reveal my victory over sexual looseness on FB under one condition: That He would **continue to keep me** on the road of sexual freedom. Although, I have been victorious over my sexual cravings for nearly two decades, I know and understand that I cannot have any confidence in my flesh *(see Philippians 3:3)*. I also know that it is nothing that I have done or could ever do that has kept me free from sexual sin for this duration of time.

After posting my sexual status on Facebook, I realized that contrary to popular belief, saved singles really do want to be free of sexual sin. Some of them just lack the know-how. The church's position on sex and the single saint doesn't appear to help the cause

2

either. It seems that when it comes to discussing the two words sex and singles in the church, the topic is almost taboo. Anytime the subject surfaces in a conversation, the exchange is usually brief. No matter the marital status of those talking about the issue of singles and sex in the church, the ultimate say-so on the topic is, "Don't do it!" Very few dare to take the topic any further. As a result single Christians suffer in silence. Single believers feel as if there is no place to talk about the who, when, what, how, and why of their sexual desire.

Don't get me wrong, I'm not bashing the church. I am so excited about how far we've progressed as a whole. Denominational and racial barriers are being broken. The church is more unified than it has ever been in the past. The Body of Christ has embraced the faith movement, prosperity message, and adopted modern day technology all in the name of sharing the gospel of Jesus Christ to the masses. While we have come a long way, evolving in areas that one would not have imagined, we still have a way to go as it pertains to talking about sex and singles in the church.

Table 1 April 12, 2013 Facebook Post

Our hush-hush has cost us big time. Instead of being the catalyst that singles run to for safety from sexual sin, the church's choice to remain distant from the matter of God's view on sex drives the single believer to the world for cover. Consequently, there is more premarital sex, same sex relationships, and children born out of wedlock in the church than there is in the world. Needless to say, this should not be.

As we talk about sex (in the church), I want to make the topics of sex, singles, and celibacy in the church a natural subject of discussion. I want the church to become so comfortable with sex that fear of the issue will be eradicated. As a result, the faith and love of God will surface to free single believers from sexual sin.

In order to experience this freedom to talk about sex (in the church), we must first become transparent. Single believers or those who aspire to become Christians don't become free from sexual sin because they feel that sex is foreign to the church. When in all actuality sex originated in the church. Sex belongs to the church. In an attempt to level the playing ground of transparency, I open up in a very honest yet sincere way about my own encounters with sexual sin. Although the process of being transparent has been a very difficult and challenging one, knowing that my story could help others makes talking about my story worth the while.

Please note that this book is based on my own experience as a nearly 20 year veteran of celibacy and sexual purity. As I mention later, once I started to pen this book I found that there are so many single Christians (both men and women) who have taken an oath of celibacy. Each individual has their own unique testimony of how God has kept them. As we talk about sex (in the church), please keep in mind that my experience is just that, "my experience."

5

While our practices may be different in how we become free from sexual sin, our principles or core beliefs, (to actually be free) should be the same. It is my prayer that you would not reinvent the whole wheel on the road to sexual freedom. I hope that you will be able to glean from my tested, tried, and true experiences of freedom over sexual sin.

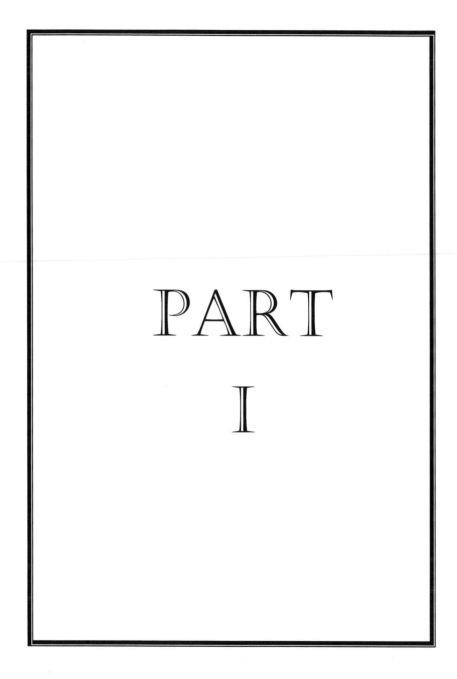

PART

I

1
Ground Rules

In order to eliminate any confusion about this book's intent or purpose, I would like to take the time to lay some basic ground rules concerning single saints and celibacy by:

1. Defining some common words associated with sex.

2. Discovering the purpose of sex as God intended it.

3. Describing the goals for this book.

4. Identifying this book's audience.

5. Exploring the reasons that single Christians have sex.

6. Encouraging single believers to come out of the closet about their choice to remain celibate.

7. Discussing the gift of Celibacy.

8. Giving a warning to the reader.

9. Thanking my audience.

Definitions	
Celibacy	To refrain from sexual intercourse until marriage. Celibacy is used interchangeably with abstinence. It is most commonly used for those who have had sex and who have chosen to stop, in order to honor God in their bodies.
Christian	*Synonym for* believer. Someone who has accepted Jesus Christ as their personal Lord and Savior according to Romans 10:8-10.
Dating	Courting between a male and female with the intent to know ones character without having sex.
Fornication	Sexual intercourse outside of marriage.
Homosexual	Sexual intercourse between two people of the same gender (two males or two females). Those who choose to practice homosexuality are also thought of as being gay.
Marriage	A covenant or union between a male and a female.
Masturbation	The arousal of one's own genitals to the point of orgasm commonly called jacking off or self-sex.
Oral Sex	The use of the mouth to arouse someone's penis or vagina. When oral sex is committed on a male it is also known as a blow job. When performed on a female, it is also defined as "eating

Definitions	
	out;" Whether performed on a male or female oral sex is also referred to as "going down on."
Orgasm	The release of sexual tension when the genitals are stimulated, also known as sexual climax.
Penis	Male sex organ.
Pornography	Pictures of sex organs and/or activity designed to arouse one sexually. These pictures are usually outside of one's husband or wife.
Promiscuity	Adjective for fornication. Denotes sexual looseness.
Sex	The involvement of any of one's members in sexual activity that includes one or more people. Including but not limited to oral sex, anal sex, pornography and/or masturbation.
Vagina	Female sex organ.
Virgin	Male or female who has never had sexual intercourse.

The Purpose Of Sex

Present of the Christian Apologetics and Research Ministry (CARM), Matthew J. Slick states that the primary purpose of sex is for a married couple (male and female) to:

1. Glorify God through procreation *(Genesis 1:28)*.
2. Experience intimacy *(Song of Solomon 1:3)*.
3. Have Companionship *(Song of Solomon 3:1)*.
4. Enjoy physical pleasure *(Song of Solomon 1:2)*.

In essence God created the sexual act for a man and a woman to identify and act like Him by continuing to make children in His image and likeness, for relational closeness, and physical pleasure (Slick, 2013).

My Goal

It is not my goal to beat anyone up about their sex lives by telling them how wrong fornication is. I am not the sex police. I do not walk around handing out sexual sin citations to everyone that I think or know is involved in sexual sin. Just like everyone else, I have to work out my own salvation (Philippians 2:12) and remain victorious over sexual sin. Becoming free from fornication was a process for me. Unless God performs a supernatural miracle (in which He can), you will experience freedom from fornication through stages also. Hopefully, because you have a proven outline (through my testimony), it will not take you as long as it took me to become free. My goal is simply to share with my reader how God delivered me from sexual sin. It is my prayer that after reading this book, you will realize that if God delivered me, He can deliver **anybody.** I hope that by sharing my story you will have the strength to walk in the victory that God has already provided for you in overcoming the lust of your flesh.

Single believers are realizing more and more that their sexual sin hurts God *(Isaiah 63:10)*, and fornication is forfeiting their right to eternal salvation and God's best while living on earth *(Revelations 21:8)*, *(I Corinthians 6:9)*. I believe for these reasons God has heard your cry to be free from the lust of the flesh. It is not my goal to condemn you, because either I was you or I could have been you. I know what it's like to feel as if my prayers cannot reach past the ceiling of my life due to the grip that sexual sin had on my life. I have cried the silent tears that you cry when nobody's looking because I did not want to hurt God, but at the same time I did not know how to press past the pain and stop sinning sexually. In "The 7-Secrets of Celibacy: The Single Christian's Guide on How to Wait on a Mate," my goal is to simply hold your hand and walk you through to the promise of freedom over promiscuity.

Audience

While anyone is encouraged to read this book and practice abstinence, it is the single Christian's obligation to live holy, sex free lives. This book is written for **single Believers and/or aspiring single Christians**. Unsaved men and women (those who have not accepted Jesus Christ as Lord and Savior) are free to do as they like with their bodies. Please note that sexual sin is not gender specific. Unlike society, God does not say that it is more acceptable for men to have sex outside of marriage than it is for women. Holy living goes for both male and female.

Yes, brothers I know that the world has made it easy and more acceptable for you to get you some (have sex) every now and then. It is even looked at as being cool for a man to have had a lot of sex. It is even cooler if he's had it with more than one partner. However, men, just because you are considered "the head" does not give you the player pass (go ahead) from God to transgress against His Word.

Reasons Single Christians Have Sex

One of the major reasons I find that single Christians are involved in illicit sex is that there is ambiguity about abstinence in the church as a whole. Singles are told what they already know, that "sex outside of marriage is wrong" and that they shouldn't be "doing it," but not many single Christians are really being helped through the process to sexual freedom. Most of the times singles are made to feel ashamed of their sexual desires.

Even single believers whose aim is to marry and do things the right way sexually are often shunned and made to feel that their desire for marriage and sex is a sign of discontent. Well-meaning believers tell single Christians things like:

> - "Just wait on the Lord."
> - "Stay single as long as you can."
> - "It will happen when you stop looking."

While all of these statements are good advice, they do very little to address the longings and desires of the single heart. Single saints are confused because they know the truth, that they shouldn't be doing it. What they lack is the "how-to" stop doing it. They are being **"told"** that sex outside of marriage is wrong but not **"showed"** (used out of context intentionally to make point) how to keep themselves sexually pure.

The truth is they don't know how to, "just wait on the Lord," stay single as long as they can, or what it means that it will happen when they stop looking. Most of them are so overwhelmed, discouraged, and frustrated with their secret sexual sin that they suffer in silence. Instead of seeking God for a solution they fulfill their sexual desire, feel bad about their actions, and walk around in a defeated and fallen state.

This vicious cycle creates a wedge between single believers and God. As a result, the single saint experiences sprinkles of

God's blessings in their lives because of His Grace. Almost unaware, they miss out on the outpouring of rain that God wants to bring into their lives. They forfeit God's best in their lives all because they have not learned the secret of reigning over their sexual natures.

Yes, whether your reason for having sex as a single Christian is:

- You're a virgin and are anxious to experiment.
- You're a veteran to sexual sin and love the way it feels
- Your biological clock is ticking and you want to have kids.
- Everybody else is doing it.
- You rationalize that God doesn't mind if you do it every now and then.

I will tell you what you already know, that all sexual activity outside of marriage is wrong. The difference that this book will make is that I want to take what you already **know** a step further and **show** you how to become free from your sexual cravings.

After reading this book you will become free to talk about sex in the church without feeling ashamed. As I open up about my own struggles on the road to victory, you will no longer have a fear of discussing your own weaknesses and viable solutions over sexual sin with other believers and/or sinners alike. Finally, you will gain the courage from my experiences to come out of sexually sin, once

16

and for all. It is my belief that if we don't teach sex in the church, saved singles will learn sex from society. Sex was and is God's idea and everything that God made is good (I Timothy 4:4).

While writing this book, I have found that there are more single Christian's that are living celibate lives than one might think. They are in the closet or in hiding for different reasons. One of the major reasons single Christians are "on the low" or in secret about their choice to remain abstinent is they don't see celibacy as being attractive.

Through the years the world and even the church has viewed those who have taken an oath of celibacy as having taken on a cloak of shame. Rather than being viewed as a badge of honor (as God intended it), single believers shun the idea of celibacy and don't want anything to do with it.

Christian women who don't have sex are thought of as old maids or rejects that no man wants. Men who live abstinent lives are called punks. What's even more shocking is this type of thinking has been adopted into the church. Consequently, we have a group of people who have embraced a sense of discontentment about their sexual and marital state. It seems that everyone wants to get married but no one wants to be single.

I want to change this perception about celibacy. I want single believers to embrace their singleness. While celibacy is about holiness, it is my belief that celibacy is sexy. Now don't go getting all religious on me, thinking that I am trying to identify celibacy with the world somehow by referring to it as being sexy. As I mentioned before, sex is of God. God did not borrow the act of sex from the world. When the world has sex, they are participating in an act that God created. When I say that celibacy is sexy, all I am saying is that sexual abstinence is attractive and to be desired. I want single Christians to come out of the closet about their choice to keep themselves sexually free, the way God intended, until marriage.

God persuades His children to be Holy for He is Holy (I Peter 1:16). I believe when He speaks of living a pure and holy life He is not requiring women to wear their dresses down to their ankles, while wearing no makeup. I also don't think He intended for men to walk around quoting scriptures 24/7, while throwing anointed oil on everyone that they come into contact with. Although, I am not against modesty or spiritual discipline, I believe that being Holy is simply about being set apart from the world. Single saints are considered Holy when they do things the way God intended, all while being their unique selves.

When single believers try to keep themselves by carrying out the manmade rules of no makeup, wearing unattractive clothes, and becoming super spiritual, they turn the unsaved off of the message of Christ. Single Christians are God's representatives and if they are not attractive then God is not attractive.

God wants to honor those who honor Him with their bodies. He wants to use celibate single saints as trophies of His goodness, mercy, and grace. In Matthew 5:15, God reminds believers not to hide their lights. He wants to use those who have made the choice to remain pure as examples to free others of their sexual sin. He wants

19

to start a celibacy movement amongst single believers, but single believers must first come out of the closet about their choice to remain celibate.

We can begin to come out of the closet about celibacy by the following:

1. Know who you are in Christ.
2. Know who God is in your life.
3. Be bold.

The Bible reminds the single believer that they are:

1. Fearfully and wonderfully made (Psalms139:14).
2. Made in God's image and likeness (Genesis 1:27).
3. Bold as lions (Psalms 28:1).

Singles cannot allow what others think of their decision to remain abstinent until marriage to cause them to waiver in their stance. Single Believers are to stand strong in their conviction about celibacy, without any apology or explanation.

No matter the need, God is the single believer's:

1. Spouse and Maker (Isaiah 54:5).

2. Friend (John 15:15).

3. Counselor (Isaiah 9:6).

4. Provider (Genesis 22:14)

5. Everything (Colossians 1:16)

Just because someone is single and celibate does not mean that they have to walk around needy and settling for less than God's best for their lives. In their time of waiting on a mate, God wants single Christians to know Him as their total fulfillment, with nothing lacking or missing. *"The 7-Secrets of Celibacy: The Single Christian's Guide on How to Wait on a Mate,"* is designed to show the single believer how to come out of the closet about the choice to remain celibate.

Knowing who one is in Christ, knowing who God is, and being bold will help the single believer to develop the fortitude needed to stand up against societal norms that say, "Celibacy is lame." Single Christians can hold their heads high during their time of waiting and be at peace with their choice. Coming out of the closet about ones choice to live celibate creates a quiet confidence that will attract others to Christ and the celibacy movement. What was once a cloak of shame is turned into a badge of honor.

The Gift Of Celibacy?

I want to emphasize that I am NOT some super spiritual Christian who has had some sort of bad sexual experience. I DO NOT hate sex. I AM NOT trying to change the world by spreading hatred toward sex. It is important to note that I DO NOT have "the gift" of celibacy or singleness that Paul speaks of in I Corinthians 7:6-9. It is said that Paul was anointed by God to remain single for the rest of his life.

I DON'T have the gift, I HAVEN'T prayed for the gift, nor do I desire the gift of celibacy. As stated before, I believe that sex was created by God and like The Word states, "Everything that God created is good," when done in the right context (I Timothy 4:4). It is important that my reader know that I have had sex, I like sex, and I look forward to having sex again, once I am married. I explain my stance on sex so that you understand the depth of my struggle and can better appreciate my victory over its grip.

WARNING To The Reader!

I think now is a good time to warn you that throughout this book I speak on subjects that some may feel is inappropriate to talk about in the church to adults, not to mention children under the age of 13. I think that our children deal with a whole lot more sexuality in school, society, and social media than we'd like to believe. For this reason, I don't feel there is such a thing as too early to begin to pray to God for timing and ways to discuss sex with our children. I talk more about how I talked to my daughter about sex in Chapter 8, "Leaving a Legacy of Celibacy: A Charge to Parents and Virgins." I think every parent knows their particular child and when is the appropriate time to talk about the subject of sex. I just want to warn you: if you plan on giving this book to a child under the age of 13 to prepare for an array of questions on the subject of sex.

While writing this book I was really concerned about what people (especially my future husband) would think of me for some of the things that I have been involved in sexually. I was apprehensive of who would not like me for my stance on sexual sin. I've even questioned if some of the topics that I talk about should really be discussed so openly.

Through much prayer, fasting, and seeking God for peace on these potential problems, I came up with the same solution. When I ask myself, "Why are you writing this book?" The answer is, "I want to help other singles who struggle with sexual sin to get to the root of their problem." It is my belief that you can't help someone if you're not willing to be transparent with them. Even though I tried to stay as tactful as possible, please **be warned** that there are instances where I am extremely open about my own experiences and to some this may be offensive.

I want you to know that it is not my desire to be offensive or tacky. I want to offer real solutions to real problems for real people. One of the reasons that I started my own book publishing company, Black Pearl Publishing, LLC was that I did not want some publishing house rejecting or limiting what I could say. I wanted to be able to say what needed to be said with the primary purpose of helping my reader. While I don't apologize for this book's contents, I want to reiterate that it is not my goal to be offensive. Please note that you have been **WARNED!**

Thank You!

Thank so much for purchasing and reading, *"The 7-Secrets of Celibacy: The Single Christian's Guide on How to Wait on a Mate."* You have taken the first step to set in motion a force of victory in your life and/or the life of your loved ones. As you read and apply the tools outlined in the following pages, get ready to experience a refreshing in your life and in the lives of those you love! Get ready to be freed from the yokes of sexual sin!

2

The Freaky 5:
Homosexuality,
Masturbation,
Oral Sex,
Sodomy
&
Pornography

W hile there are a lot of different types of Sex that single believers are involved in that include:

- Sexual fantasies
- Pornography
- Masturbation
- Oral sex
- Sexting
- Phone sex
- Vaginal
- Anal
- Sodomy
- Fingering
- Rimming
- Homosexuality
- Bestiality

I want to reemphasize that any sex outside of the marriage covenant is sin. Some of the previous categories of sex are considered outright abominations (in or outside of marriage). With so many alternatives to sex as God intended it, I could not leave out the topic of what I have coined, *"The Freaky 5."* They are **Homosexuality, Masturbation, Oral Sex, Sodomy,** and **Pornography.** You would think that Single Christians would know better than to be involved in such things. I should be able to skip the subject and move on to other issues, but the Freaky 5 are just as prevalent in the lives of single believers as they are in the world.

Headlines are full of stories about gay marriages in churches around the world. Somehow it has become ok to buy the latest sex gadgets to pacify one's sexual longings. Oral sex and sodomy have become as common as the latest fad or fashion amongst single saints, and you can hardly cut the television on without seeing people in the nude in some form or fashion. The truth is these acts should not be found in the marriage covenant let alone in the lives of the single believer. Let's take a look at each of The Freaky 5 individually in respect to God's Word to see what I mean.

Homosexuality

Who exchanged the truth of God for the lie, and worshiped and served the creature rather than the Creator, who is blessed forever. Amen.

For this reason God gave them up to vile passions. For even their women exchanged the natural use for what is against nature. Likewise also the men, leaving the natural use of the woman, burned in their lust for one another, men with men committing what is shameful, and receiving in themselves the penalty of their error which was due.

27

And even as they did not like to retain God in their knowledge, God gave them over to a debased mind, to do those things which are not fitting; being filled with all unrighteousness, sexual immorality, wickedness, covetousness, maliciousness; full of envy, murder, strife, deceit, evil-mindedness; they are whisperers, backbiters, haters of God, violent, proud, boasters, inventors of evil things, disobedient to parents, undiscerning, untrustworthy, unloving, unforgiving, unmerciful; who, knowing the righteous judgment of God, that those who practice such things are deserving of death, not only do the same but also approve of those who practice them (Romans 1:25-32)

I know that there are some deep rooted issues that involve people who think that they were born gay or are attracted to those of the same sex. In the majority of the cases that involve homosexuality that I know about, there has been a basic common thread in each instance that includes:

- Unresolved parental pain.
- A sexual violation from someone of the same gender.
- Simple curiosity or experimentation.

I've witnessed men who have estranged relationships with their Fathers, try and fill that void through a homosexual relationship. I have also seen women who have a rocky relationship with their Father, but a good relationship with their Mother, gravitate toward a homosexual relationship. It's almost as if the homosexual relationship is more comfortable to them. In my upcoming book, "From Pain to Reign in My Window: My Victory over Fatherlessness©," I discuss how important the parental relationship is in the development of all other relationships in a child's life. I tell how, when the parental relationship is unstable, (without proper repair) it causes all other relationships to be off balance in the child's life.

The Law of First Mention

Before I discuss the most common case that I am familiar with between same sex relationships, I want to take a moment to briefly address the thousands if not millions of people who feel as if they were born gay. These individuals state that they have always been attracted to same sex relationships and have embraced the erroneous concept that being gay is how God created them. I also want to state that I am aware that not all people who practice homosexuality have been abused sexually or have terrible relationships with their parents.

I don't intend to get into great debates over the reasons that people practice homosexuality while missing the reality of God's

29

Word. God clearly states in His Word that homosexuality is wrong. You should also know that I am not a homophobe. I am not afraid of being around those who practice homosexuality, as I am very comfortable with my own sexuality. I have both family and friends who openly and secretly practice homosexuality. None of these things are important to me. This book is not about why people practice homosexuality. It is about honoring God by remaining abstinent until one is married to someone of the opposite sex. The only reason that I address the topic is because homosexuality is a major type of sex practiced by single Christians today. Just as sex with a heterosexual before marriage is wrong, homosexuality is immoral in or outside of the marriage bed and needs to be addressed.

"And Jehovah God said, it is not good that the man should be alone; I will make him a help meet for him... and Jehovah God caused a deep sleep to fall upon the man, and he slept; and he took one of his ribs, and closed up the flesh instead thereof: and the rib, which Jehovah God had taken from the man, made He a woman, and brought her unto the man. And the man said, this is now bone of my bones, and flesh of my flesh: she shall be called Woman, because she was taken out of man. Therefore shall a man leave his father and his mother, and shall cleave unto his wife: and they

shall be one flesh. And they were both naked, the man and his wife, and were not ashamed." (Genesis 2:18, 19-25 American Standard Version)

This passage exhibits what Bible scholars call the Law of First Mention of marriage in scripture. The law of first mention is where a principle is set in God's Word that "Requires one to go to that portion of the scriptures where a doctrine is mentioned for the first time and to study the first occurrence of the same in order to get the fundamental inherent meaning of that doctrine" (Cooper & Haynie).

Another way to think of the Law of First Mention is to view it as a blueprint for all other occurrences after it. In this particular passage God put Adam to sleep, conducted the first operation and created Eve using one of his ribs. When Adam's anesthesia wore off and he came out of surgery, at first sight he called Eve woman because she was taken from him (man).

The passage goes on to explain that a man should leave his father and mother and cleave to his wife, making the two one. The Hebrew meaning of cleave means to be "closely pursued," or "be deeply attracted" (The Lockman Foundation, 1981, 1988). According to the Law of First Mention, God clearly intended for Adam (man) to closely pursue, and become deeply attracted to Eve (woman). This act would fulfill what we know today as, the marriage covenant. I don't know if God's guidelines for the marriage and or sex can be any simpler. God clearly intended for

31

marriage to be between one man and one woman, according to the Law of First Mention.

Experimentation

Other reasons that people get involved with homosexuality is because:

- Same sex relationships have become so acceptable in our culture that the church has numbed its heart to God's Word on the subject.
- The orgasmic experience is so thrilling that those who explore homosexuality through curiosity or who have been sexually violated are convinced that they are gay (especially if the first orgasm that they experience is with someone of the opposite sex).

The primary reason that I can relate to why people get involved with homosexuality is because of simple experimentation or curiosity. While I have **NEVER** been romantically attracted to someone of the same sex, I can *identify* with how one can be tricked into thinking that they are gay or become infatuated with a same sex relationship.

Child's Play

As a child I used to go over a friend's house to play at about age 11 or 12 years of age. She and I would go to her room and talk. For some reason there was a period of time that she began to make advances at me (for those of you who know me and my best friend throughout Junior High, High School, and adulthood, this is **NOT** that friend). As I look back, I believe that someone was violating her sexually and she was acting out their behavior with me.

Even though I felt extremely violated and ashamed about the encounter, I had not yet developed a voice to say no. With all of her clothes on she would without saying anything get on top of me and begin to gyrate. I will discuss later in Part II, The 7-Secrets, how I was violated by some adult men in my childhood. Oddly enough her behavior felt somewhat familiar to me, even though she was a girl. I don't remember saying anything and I vaguely remember moving but one time while she moved on top of me, I was stimulated to an orgasm for the first time. I did not know or understand the feeling that I experienced at that time, but I remember the feeling being so invigorating, yet scary for me that I quit going to her house. I never talked to her or anyone else about the incident until recently, but I knew enough at the time to know that this was not an experience that I should be having with even a boy (at this age), not to mention a girl. Though it felt good to my body, my heart somehow knew that it was wrong.

Because of this experience, as I grew older and began to encounter gay relationships, I could understand how a person could think that they were gay through curiosity and experimentation. I also realized that had it not been for the grace of God and having strong women around me in the form of my Mom, Grandmother, and aunts that I could have easily been confused about this feeling and been attracted to women.

Unlike me, I believe there are a lot of adults who got hooked on same sex relationships through sheer curiosity and/or experimentation. I don't know if homosexuality is more difficult to overcome than heterosexuality but I do know that God is bigger than any sin. The same way that He delivers those who practice fornication with those of the opposite sex, He will deliver you.

Masturbation

Masturbation is so common among saved single believers because it does not involve the penetration of the penis into the vagina or the participation of another individual. This causes those single Christians who practice self-sex to feel somewhat justified by their actions because they don't think that they are offending God.

Of all of the arguments that I have heard about masturbation being okay with God, I think the most farfetched reason that I've heard is the one that claims that God allows masturbation to keep Christians away from sexual sin with another human. God plainly tells the believer "Nevertheless, because of sexual immorality, let each man have his own wife, and let each woman have her own husband" *(I Corinthians 7:2)*. Here The Bible sums up the context in which God intended sex: with one's OWN WIFE or HUSBAND (in a heterosexual relationship). This verse eliminates tools/objects, another's husband or wife, animals, one's hand, and anything else outside one's OWN WIFE or HUSBAND.

The whole premise for "The 7-Secrets of Celibacy: The Single Christians Guide on How to Wait on a Mate," is about having a relationship with God so that He can give you a clear understanding of who He is and what He expects. This is not about finding loopholes to fulfill the desires of the flesh.

When single Christian's involve themselves in masturbation they are making get-outs for the flesh to live unholy. No, The Bible does not come outright and say thou shall not commit masturbation. Believers are encouraged to ask God when unsure about any situation (James 1:5). This includes wisdom about what is considered right and wrong during sex. When God gives you the answer, don't dismiss it because it is not pleasing to your flesh.

Yes, during my time of sexual experimentation, I have practiced masturbation. I must say that at the end of the act, while I did experience an orgasmic release, I have NEVER felt good about myself. Self-sexual penetration always made me feel dirty, ashamed, and embarrassed of myself. Instead of continuing in the sin of masturbation, I have had to use the same tools that I discuss throughout this book to become free.

35

The Sin Of Onan

While there are saved singles that practice masturbation who want to get married, there are also a remnant of believers that practice masturbation because they do not want to get married and/or have kids. For whatever reason, these individuals have not harnessed their sexual cravings. Instead of seeking God for freedom from lust, they masturbate to escape the responsibility that comes along with doing things God's way. This group becomes like Onan who instead of fulfilling his duty to "Raise up Seed" for his brother he chose to have sex with his brother's wife, (enjoy the act of sex) without having the responsibility of bearing a child in his brother's honor.

This is selfish on every level. The Word of God says that "his actions displeased God". What I would like to suggest to you is: If you are practicing masturbation because you don't want to get married and/or rear children then you are committing the sin of Onan and are likewise, "Displeasing God." Onan could have said no to the request of his father. I think his "No" would have been more honorable than having sex and not following through on his commitment by spilling his seed.

Likewise, if you do not want to get married or have children, why not ask God for the "Gift of Celibacy" that Paul had where he did not know a woman. I think this be more honorable to God than you gratifying yourself without having the responsibility of having to have a spouse and/or children. When we become born again and say that we love God, our lives are not our own. We say, "No" to our way of doing things and taking care of ourselves (including sexually) and "Yes" to God.

Oral Sex

There is a huge controversy as to whether oral sex should even be performed in the confines of marriage, let alone in the lives of single Christians. Okay, okay, okay, I have a confession to make! To be honest, initially (probably up until the time this book was ready for circulation), I was going to play it safe and remain in the middle of the road about oral sex. Because I didn't have (or should I say, I didn't want) a personal revelation from God about oral sex being right or wrong to practice in marriage, I wasn't going to even go there. This changed when I talked to one of my married friends who reminded me that my Pastor and First Lady, Drs.' Ron and Georgette Frierson strongly denounce oral sex during our yearly marriage retreats.

Yes, I knew my leaders stance on the subject. They have taught that oral penetration is wrong during our singles sessions as well. Like many singles and married people alike, because it is not clearly noted in The Bible that oral sex is wrong, I wasn't settled on the stance of my spiritual parents. I have heard noteworthy pastors teach that oral sex is wrong and should not be practiced in the marriage bed. I have also heard prominent preachers say it's okay

37

to have oral sex, just as long as it is between a married couple (man and woman), and consensual between both parties. Because this is a book for singles and not a marriage book and I was 100% certain that single believers should not be going down on one another to fulfill their fleshly lusts, I was going to just leave the discussion at, "Single Christian's should not be having oral sex."

I also know my flesh and that oral sex was an experience that I enjoyed during my time of sexual activity. The question that kept plaguing my thoughts over the years was, "Is oral sex of God?" No matter how settled I tried to become about oral sex being right in marriage, it just never felt right in my spirit. (*This is not to say that sex in the confines of marriage shouldn't be enjoyable. As I stated before, sex is one of the most beautiful experiences known to man and woman*). The point that I am trying to make is that because something feels good sexually (*or otherwise*), does not mean that it's of God. I often jokingly tell friends that, "By the time I figured out what I thought was fun during sex, God was nudging me to quit."

After hearing my leader's position on oral sex I have had great debates with God about His meaning on the topic. I gave Him His Word that He said, the marriage bed is undefiled, *Hebrews 13:4.* I took this scripture to mean that anything goes in the marriage bed as long as The Bible does not preach against it.

I embraced the idea that as long as both the husband and wife are in agreement with oral sex or does not have any objections to the activity then it was all good to perform. I closed my heart to any other information that would be contrary to this definition because it was what I liked. I always told God that I would participate in oral sex once I got married no matter what anyone else thought. At the same time, I half-heartedly agreed to remain open to correction if God gave me a personal revelation that my train of thought was in error.

As my friend gave me the spill about oral sex being sin (along with the Romans 1:25-32 Bible verse often used to defend the argument), I subtly tuned her out. I was going to practice oral sex once I was married and that was final, until the Lord brought up the subject of sodomy during my prayer time.

Sodomy

Following the chat with my friend about oral sex, I decided to read the infamous scripture in Romans 1:25-32. I was at peace with the fact that I had, what I thought was the green light from God to have oral sex when I got married. After reading the scripture, I began to meditate on this Chapter of the book. I was originally going to entitle this chapter HMOS; which is the acronym for Homosexuality, Masturbation, and Oral Sex.

Even though I felt a sense of vulnerability for talking about my own experiences with each of the topics, I could also sense a level of pride about the subjects as I felt that I had been obedient to God with my transparency. I was satisfied with the fact that I had been open and honest with bearing my soul. I had put everything on the floor concerning my experience with each topic and was sure that God was pleased, until God began to talk to me about Sodomy and Pornography.

"Sodomy?" I said to God.

"You can't want me to talk about Sodomy in this book. God I have told all of my business in this book. This book is for the church, and I am a Christian. Why would You want me to bring sodomy up?"

Yes, I like a lot of people have experienced some very perverted sex in my life time!

The Word vs. The World

As I began to think about why single Christians dabble in such perversion when it comes to sex, I realize the answer is found in the world. Most single Christians have been in the world longer than they have been in The Word. It seems almost automatic that they have adopted many of the world's ways, without knowing that they are grieving God with their actions. Even in the marriage covenant the world says, the freakier you are the better you are in bed. The Word says the holier you are the better you are in bed (see IPeter1:16). The world says you have to do what it takes to turn your partner out in order to keep him or her. The world's mindset is to put it (sex) on them so good that they will not be able to even think about someone else, no less have sex with another person.

40

The world wants to keep their partner happy by any means necessary, even if it means dishonoring God. In Romans 12 we are encouraged by the Apostle Paul to "be not conformed to this world but be ye transformed by the renewing of your mind" (Romans 12:1). I know that even some married straight couples may not agree that three of The Freaky 5 (masturbation, oral sex and sodomy) are in fact sin because they are appealing to the flesh. But as previously stated, just because something feels good does not make it pleasing to God.

Again, I am not saying that sex should not be fun, exciting, and pleasing with ones husband or wife. What I want you to do as a believer is take everything you do in and outside of the marriage bed to God and ask Him how He feels about it. I believe that any sin ties God's hands in blessing His people. It is my earnest belief that God cannot take some marriages to higher levels, either spiritually, naturally and/or sexually because perverted sex has tied His hands on their behalf. As a result, I think that some married couples are missing out on the BEST sex of their lives because they are ignorantly or knowingly doing things the world's way instead of The Words way.

If you are offended by this chapter and feel like who do I think that I am telling people what they can and can't do in the marriage bed, then, I am especially talking to you. When we are doing what is right in God's eyes and someone is telling us different we usually don't get upset with others for their stance. While we may not agree with what the other person is saying, we can dismiss

41

it with a clear conscience. Your offense and lack of peace shows that you may need to get with God on what He thinks about what you are doing behind closed doors.

I told you previously that I had been violated by trusted men in my life. Besides causing me to feel somewhat comfortable with being molested, being violated also caused me to adopt the idea that the only way to please a man was in bed. This thought pattern gave me the false perception that if I performed like a freak in bed that he would be so far gone and overwhelmed by his sexual experience with me that he would not ever think about someone else or want someone other than me.

God began to remind me of our sexual culture and how it has gotten worse since I had retired from sexual sin. If I was involved with the types of sex that I had been involved with nearly two decades ago, there is no telling what young people are experiencing today. If my true goal is to help men and women to become free then I would have to tell it all, holding nothing back and being totally transparent.

Unnatural Function

While doing a casual research of the act of sodomy, I conducted a simple Google search and was nearly floored by the online definition that the Merriam-Webster dictionary gave me. According to Merriam-Webster sodomy is "**anal** or **oral** copulation with a member of the same or opposite sex; also: **copulation with an animal**." (Merriam-Webster, 2014)

"Whoa!" I thought. If sodomy (which I knew was an abomination to The Word of God) is synonymous to **anal, oral,** or **bestial** intercourse, then it's true that oral sex is sin. This was enough for me. Although some may disagree, The Church does not usually argue much about sodomy or bestiality being sin. We all know the story of how God destroyed Sodom and Gomorrah because the sin of the people was a great "outcry against them" (read Genesis 19:1-28). Romans 1:26 speaks of women exchanging the natural function for that which is unnatural. Ask any physician and you will be told that the anus was not meant for insertion and that insertion into the anus could cause great medical damage. Whether in a heterosexual marriage or homosexual union, sex in the anus is an **unnatural function**.

When I got the understanding that oral sex was just as wrong as anal sex or even worse, **bestiality,** I honestly thought, "Forget it! I don't even want to get married now! I mean, why get married if you can't have fun in bed with your mate?" As I continued to take my concerns about oral sex to God, He began to change my immature thought pattern and little by little I was able to embrace how having sex The Word's way instead of the world's way would allow me to fulfill God in my marriage.

Pornography

But I say to you that whoever looks at a woman to lust for her has already committed adultery with her already in his heart."

Matthew 5:28

Pornography generally isn't thought of as sex because it doesn't require genital penetration. Those single Christian's who are involved in pornography may argue that because this sexual act is only committed in the mind, they have not sinned. Matthew 5:28 tells us that if we even look at a woman (or man) to lust we've committed adultery in our hearts (emphasis mine).

"Geesh," you may be thinking. "I am inundated with sexually suggestive visuals on a daily basis. How am I supposed to keep myself from pornographic sin?"

Unless we plan to lock ourselves in a cell for the rest of our lives, it is nearly impossible to keep ourselves completely from pornography. Pictures that are sexual in nature are hung on billboards everywhere. All one has to do is log into a social media site to get mobbed by unwanted pornography. Friends and family forward unsolicited sexual emails and texts. The pornography industry has even found ways to send sexually suggestive e-mails to innocent subscribers without their consent.

Subtle Porn

While the average single saint would not involve themselves in what is called the hard core pornography of watching X-rated movies or visiting a ladies or gentleman's club, they must still guard themselves from what I call subtle porn. Subtle porn is where one is forced to look at sexually explicit visuals usually by outsiders, without warning. It could also mean being reminded of a past sexual experience through these visuals. This could be a picture of a woman in a swim suit at work, a man exposing his penis on a Facebook post, or a so called friend sending an X-rated text that they think is funny. These things are far from funny. They are pornographic and a form of having sex, in the mind.

God requires the believer to love Him with all of their hearts, all of their minds, and all of their strength (see Luke 10:27). You can't love God with your mind if it is full of sexually explicit pictures. One day The Lord spoke to me, "What you allow to go on in your head, you will allow to go on in your life." If you allow pornographic images to fill your head, it won't be long before the thought is planted, rooted, watered and made manifest. If you are not prayerful and careful, you could find yourself acting the thought out.

In my BC (Before Christ) days, I have watched hard core pornography. Because the images excited me sexually, it wasn't long before I was trying to pacify my sexual urges by having sex, even if through masturbation.

Some of my friends playfully joke with me today because I don't make it a habit of watching movies that are above a PG-13 rating. I'm not a huge TV fan anyway, but in an effort to guard my heart and starve my sexual appetite, I stay away from R and X-Rated films. There are some exception to R ratings, but I don't watch anything X-Rated or above (XX or XXX- if there is even such a thing)

Like me, the average Christian will not watch an X-rated movie, but there are some believers who have no regard for watching PG-13 and R- rated films that are heavy with sexual content. I call these types of movies, "Subtle Porn."

Subtle Vs. Hard Core Porn

In an X-rated movie you know what to expect. Those who have watched X-rated movies know that within the first 5 seconds of the film, the actors will be tearing off their clothes and performing more sexual tricks than a well-orchestrated circus act. After the conclusion of the movie onlookers are so hot, bothered, and sexually stirred that they want nothing more than sexual release.

"Subtle Porn" is a little different than hard core pornography. With "Subtle Porn" you don't normally see it coming. The sexual image or past sexual experience kind of sneaks upon you. For example, I love dating myself. Although I have four

46

biological siblings and grew up with a host of cousins that I consider my brothers and sisters, I was raised in a single parent home as an only child. Being an only child has taught me how to enjoy spending time alone in what I call my, "Me time." I have no problem eating alone, traveling alone, or going to see a movie alone. In fact, I LOVE it!

On one of my "Date Nights, With Me Nights" (Time that I take often to date myself), I went to see the movie, "The Best Man Holiday." The movie starred actor, Morris Chestnut and a host of other notable performers. I did my normal check and asked a few people who saw the movie some questions to see if it was ok that I watch. As always they told me of the sexual pros and cons and I made the decision to go see the R rated film, alone.

While I loved, loved, loved the overall story line and the movie as a whole, I have to tell you that I was caught off guard by a particular sex scene. Because I have been celibate for nearly 20 years, I don't normally trip over sex scenes in a movie. If a sex scene surfaces while I am watching a PG-13 or R rated movie, no problem. I either get up for a popcorn/bathroom break or close my eyes until the scene passes, and I'm good. No problem.

This particular scene in "The Best Man Holiday" somehow "trapped" me. It was as if my mind went back and I was there in the scene! The scene was where Robyn and Harper played by actors Sanaa Lathan and Taye Diggs were husband and wife. The couple was pregnant. During this particular scene the two were having sex.

There was little if any skin shown but what through me off was the personal familiarity of the scene.

I stopped having sex a few years after I had my daughter. In the common sex position for those who are pregnant, Harper laid behind Robyn holding her in all the right places, doing and saying all the right things. Even the look in his eyes took me there!

Lawd! Lawd! Lawd! I couldn't close my eyes; I couldn't get up and run for a popcorn break! I was trapped in "Subtle Porn!" Because me and all of my ex's have moved on, and I guard my heart from sexual fantasies, I was really surprised at how this scene affected me. I felt so bad about the experience that after the movie I had to take some specific steps to put my flesh under. The actions I took to bring myself back around after this occurrence at the theater was:

1. I Ran to Jesus.
2. Repented for placing myself in the reach of "Subtle Porn."
3. Renewed my mind in God's word.

So many times when singles sin sexually, instead of running to God for help they block their chance for freedom by running from God for their deliverance. This leads them to stay in sexual sin longer than they have to. Repenting to God doesn't always mean that you will never commit that particular sin again. What repentance does is tell God that you are sorry for sinning against His Word, and you will not knowingly practice that sin again because you are willing to implore His help to stop. Many people don't repent out of fear of repeating their sin. They feel that they are being fake if they repent of sin and then turn around and repeat the same sin.

When a believer repents of sexual or any other sin, they are really displaying humility towards God. Repentance says, "God I'm sorry for sinning and I need your help to overcome sin." God understands this process of repentance: confessing and asking God for help to overcome. If He can get single believers to understand this, instead of running from Him when they sin sexually, He could deliver them by getting them to run to Him. When the single believer runs to God after they've messed up God can renew their minds as He gives them His word on deliverance.

Unlike X-rated movies you don't expect to be triggered sexually. "Subtle Porn" sneaks up on you unannounced, triggering an old relationship, and before you know it, you are there sexually in your mind.

If you are going to keep yourself sexually pure there are some practical steps to take to keep you from getting caught in the trap of subtle porn:

> ■ Pray before you go to a movie. Although I prayed before going to see "The Best Man Holiday," I ignored some of the signs that would have cautioned

49

me. Because I heard all of the reviews that said it was a great movie, I just wanted to see it. My friends and family told me that there were some sex scenes in the movie, but all I heard was that it had a great story line.

- Read the ratings before you go to a movie. Not all movies are Rated R because they have sexual scenes. Some are rated R due the violent nature of the film. Reading the ratings and reviews will help you to know what you're getting yourself into before you get into it.

- Stay accountable. I don't usually tell a lot of people where I am going when I go somewhere alone. Not because I don't want accountability, but my friends and family love me. Sometimes if they hear that I am going someplace alone they try and talk me out of it or offer to have other people to tag along when I truly need to be alone. Usually I only tell my Mother, daughter and a trusted friend or two that I am going to a movie. I tell them where I am going because I know that I will be asked how I liked the movie, and I will have to tell on myself if something in the movie is not right.

As a reminder, if you or someone you know gets caught in the trap of either "Hard Core Pornography" or what I call, "Subtle Porn," do not beat yourself or loved one up. Free yourself and/or loved one by doing what I did:

1. Run to God.
2. Repent of your sin.
3. Renew your mind with the Word of God.

I still know some of you are thinking that I am just too saved, too deep, and/or too holy. You've made up in your mind that you are going to do what you want to do, and that's okay. I want to leave you with this: Is doing what you want to do worth not having God's best? Is being in a homosexual relationship, practicing masturbation, oral sex, anal sex, sodomy, and/or pornography worth you living a substandard life or even worse going to hell for? Please stay open to God, teachable, and ready to change even when it challenges your flesh.

Don't be like I was. Don't be in the middle of the road in your relationship with God as it pertains to what types of sex is pleasing to Him, because you want to gratify your flesh. If you can't get with this section or any sections of the book right now, continue to question God's Word with a heart that says, "God, I want to please You. I can live without The Freaky 5 (homosexuality, masturbation, oral sex, sodomy, and/or pornography), but I cannot live without a true relationship and fellowship with You."

While the world should be copying the churches example of sexual purity, the church is impersonating the world's lascivious lifestyles. Whether you have deep rooted issues as to why you struggle with the strong hold of a same sex attraction or if you are a product of experimentation and/or curiosity, maybe you practice masturbation because you honestly didn't think that it was sin, or you just don't want to get married and/or have kids, or if you are involved in sodomy because you think it's what you have to do to get and keep your lover.

Whatever your reasons are for practicing any or all of The Freaky 5, I don't want to condemn or judge you. I want to persuade you to use The 7-Secrets of Celibacy and the prayers that are found at the end of this book to overcome all sexual sin.

3

Wrap it
Before You Tap it...
Safe Sex?

Safe Sex

After "The Freaky Five" chapter, "Safe sex" is probably the last topic that you would think about when discussing abstinence or celibacy. To tell the truth, I went back and forth about rather I should put this chapter in the book. The more I thought about it, the more I realized that I would be amiss if I didn't talk about what the world considers, "safe sex." I want to reiterate, this entire book is about having God's best in your life and God's best is "**NO SEX**;" until marriage.

However, I do realize that some people (young and old are going to "get them some" or have sex before they are married. No matter what God, me, or anybody else says, there are those single Christian's who are just going to get it in (period). God is a gentleman and will not force us to do anything that we do not want to do. He made us free moral agents with the ability to exercise our power of choice. That's why He encourages us in Deuteronomy 30:19 to choose life so that we and our seed can live.

With that being said, if you are one of those people who choose to have sex before you get married, it should be what the world calls, "safe sex." Please keep in mind that the only real "safe sex" before marriage is "no sex." Yes, I am saying if you insist on doing things your own way by indulging in the sexual sin, then you should use contraceptives. Does this stance contradict everything else we've talked about up until this point? No, it only allows you to exercise your choice. Let me explain.

I have noticed a common thread among single men and women in today's culture. Sinner or Saint, a lot of Men no longer fill the traditional role in a relationship of pursuer, provider, protector, and priest. Most women have misplaced their roles as mother, nurturer, and one to be pursued all in the name of women's rights. This loss in identities has caused singles to settle in the area of commitment in a romantic relationship. As a result, singles as a whole have abandoned the covenant of marriage.

After noticing this trend, I made a comment on Facebook that women (especially teens), who are going to practice sex (outside of marriage), needed to make brothers, "Wrap it before he taps it," or practice what the world considers "safe sex." This statement offended some of my friend base in the church. They felt as if I was watering down God's Word and giving young ladies the go ahead to have sex outside of marriage. I want to share with you what I shared with a sister who did not understand where I was coming from with this statement.

Teen pregnancy has sky rocketed over the years, especially in the church. Being a single mother, I know how difficult it is to raise a child alone. No matter if you are a man or woman and no matter how involved the other parent is in the child's life, single parenthood is **NO JOKE**! For this reason, it is my belief that if you just insist on making a choice to have sex before you're married, you should "wrap it before you tap it," or use birth control. Again, I encourage unmarried men and women who are having sex to use contraceptives to prevent unwanted pregnancy.

You Have A Choice

"I call heaven and earth as witnesses today against you, that I have I set before you life and death, blessing and cursing; therefore choose life that both you and your descendants can live" (Deuteronomy 30:19).

While I would NEVER give anybody a license to sin, if it is what they want, they are going to sin anyway. I think some in the church have fallen short in meeting people where they are, until they get to where God wants them to be. As stated before, God gives us a choice (Deuteronomy 30:19). Until people get to the point where they can make proper choices, they have to stop doing things that they will regret for the rest of their lives while expecting others to pick up the slack.

Parents of teens are forced to take care of grandchildren that their kids are not able to provide for either financially or emotionally. Single adults have to juggle kids from family member to family member to try and provide safe childcare while they go to work to put a roof over the child's head. In addition, some young ladies are left stuck with babies on the welfare system. Young men are left with outstanding child support balances that they cannot afford to pay. This is all because neither was aware, or didn't care, about the impact that their choice to have sex had on their lives or the lives of those around them.

57

In return, they become victims of circumstance. Some women become bitter at men because one man didn't meet all of their misguided expectations. These single women feel let down when their child's father does not stick by them and their child. Men blame the woman for "trapping" him with a kid that he is forced to pay child support for. This vicious cycle causes individuals to become overwhelmed with defeat.

I know that there are some underlying issues that contribute to teen and adult sex outside of marriage. Some are trying to fill voids and want to belong. Others are seeking identity through sexual intercourse. It's true, these matters need to be addressed. But until singles are mature enough to deal with these problems, they should be told to use protection before having sex.

However, those of you who have your minds made up to remain in or get involved with premarital sex, you should know that there are some consequences and repercussions for your choice. While condoms, birth control pills, implants and other contraceptives decrease the chance of childbirth and sexually transmitted disease, none of these precautions are designed to heal the heart, spirit, and soul once they are broken due to the act of illicit sex. It is imperative that you know the spiritual, emotional, and natural consequences associated with your resolve to have sex before marriage.

Spiritual Consequences

Spiritually, sexual sin separates single Christians from God *(I Corinthians 6:9)*. Not only do they risk eternal damnation when they practice sex outside of marriage, but they forfeit kingdom living here on the earth. To top it all off, their prayers are hindered, as they are not heard and cannot be answered by God *(John 9:31)*. When believers have sex outside of marriage their souls are joined or knit to the soul of their sex partner(s) *(Mark 10:8)*. They commit sin against their own bodies *(I Corinthians 6:18)* and overall they end up with a fragmented soul and broken life.

Sexual intercourse before marriage puts saved saints in jeopardy of always needing another person to fulfill them. The more sex that they have outside of marriage, the needier they become. Because sex is such a beautiful experience, they become attached to the false notion that when they have sex, they have found love. Because sex or anything else (outside of God) was ever meant to completely fulfill them, they become emotionally attached, thinking they need more sex to be fulfilled.

Emotional Consequences

The emotional damage caused by fornication is unlimited. Sexual sin is the formula for emotional disaster. When a single person's soul becomes one with their sex partner and each of their partners, if the relationship is up those involved are on an emotional high. On the contrary, if the relationship is down, they are not only down, they are down and out. I think there is more teen and adult suicides, depression, and drug use among persons that are sexually active than instances where sexual sin is not present. When you have sex before marriage, it places a single believer's emotions in the hands of happenstance because they are emotionally tied (through sexual intercourse) to someone who is not their husband or wife. A single saint is required to be sober minded and stable where their emotions are concerned, *(I Peter 5:8)*. When they disregard God's Word as it pertains to sex, they become intoxicated in their emotions and are not able to make clear headed decisions about their lives.

Natural Consequences

The obvious natural repercussions of sexual sin are sexually transmitted diseases also known as STD'S that can be contracted. With or without protection, having sex before marriage increases a singles Christian's chance of catching a sexually transmitted disease such us Herpes, Aids, Gonorrhea, and a host of other diseases in which most are incurable (outside of a miracle from God). Other natural consequences of sexual sin are that it delays God's best in your life in the area of a mate, and chaos in every other area of your existence. Sexual sin, like any other sin, opens the door for the devil to run rampant in the life of the single Christian. Allow God to purge you so that you can experience the manifestation of His best in every area of life.

Considerations

I know how this Chapter may seem to contradict the goal of celibacy that is at the heart of this entire book. I felt that I could not write a book about celibacy without addressing the group of people who are going to do what they want sexually, no matter what. This chapter should not be used as a scapegoat for parents or children to use contraceptives and have sex with everything that moves. We have a responsibility to keep our temples. People perish for a lack of knowledge *(Hosea 4:6)*. This section's main objective is to give you knowledge and understanding on the sexual choices that you have and the consequences that come along with those choices. I discuss more in-depth ways in which one can keep themselves sexually pure in Section III for both teens and adults. "Leaving a Legacy of Celibacy: A charge to Parents and Virgins" is designed to help parents mentor children through a lifestyle of abstinence by keeping their virginity until marriage.

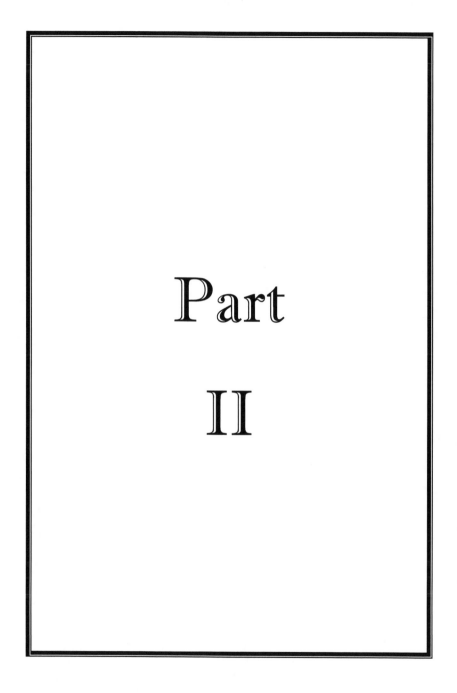

Part

II

1

My Journey

Seeking God For Solutions

My journey to abstinence began in 1996 during my third year of Salvation when I started to feel defeated in almost every area of my Christian life. My self-esteem was low, I was uneducated and living below the poverty level. My relationship with my boyfriend (at the time) was on the rocks, and everything that I tried in life looked as if it had failed. As I began to seek God for solutions, He began to speak to my heart about abstinence.

In the crevices of my mind, I knew that sexual sin was eating away at any chance that I had at a victorious life in Christ. Like a lot of singles, I wanted to find a loop hole around the subject. The matter was extra difficult for me because I was in love with my ex-boyfriend and I thought that having sex was one of the ways that I showed my love.

During a teary and emotional conversation with God about the direction that my relationship with my ex was headed was the first time that I would allow God to talk to me about sexual sin. I could not understand how a relationship with someone that I once adored and who also once adored me, could get so off course the way that my ex and I had.

What God would speak to my spirit next, would change my life and how I would view sexual sin, forever.

Love Or Lust?

"You've got to quit sleeping with him. What makes you different from unsaved women who are giving it up?" God asked.

In a desperate attempt to be justified, I bawled back at God, "But I love him!"

God gently yet firmly responded, "If you love him, you will quit sleeping with him. You are the only example of God that he may ever know. If you say that you are a Christian and you continue to sleep with him, you show him that it's okay that Christians fornicate. You don't love him, you lust him. The parameters of my love are in I Corinthians 13:4-8,

> *Love is patient and kind, never jealous or envious,*
> *never boastful or proud. Love is never haughty or*
> *selfish or rude. Love does not demand its own way.*
> *Love is not irritable or touchy. Love does not hold*
> *grudges and will hardly even notice when others do*
> *it wrong. Love is never glad about injustice, but*
> *rejoices whenever truth wins out. If you love him,*
> *you will be loyal to him no matter what the costs.*
> *You will always believe in him, always expect the*
> *best in him, and will always stand your ground in*
> *defending him.*

That is how you are to love him (God continued). If you love him, you will train his child in the fear and admonition of the Lord. If you love him you will want to see him saved. If he were to die right now, he would go to hell and his blood would be on your hands."

At that moment, it was as if a light bulb had come on in my head. For the first time, I understood that real love, God's love wants GOD'S best for others, no matter if it gets what it wants from the other person or not.

God continued, "If you will quit sleeping with him, I will save him."

I immediately pulled myself together: I dried my tears and wiped my nose. I walked away from that conversation with God with a new found purpose and direction: To love my ex with God's love. I had this discussion with God on a Friday, when that Sunday came around my ex was at church giving his life to the Lord, without any prodding from me. Although he and I never got back together, and our break up was extremely painful for me, at least, I experienced a peace that I still don't understand.

This encounter with God taught me how to love in a way that I had not known up until that point: Unconditionally. I was able to walk away from the relationship knowing that my life and my daughter's life would be better for it. I also knew that no matter what happened between us, my ex's life would be blessed as well. Just knowing that I was honoring God, myself, my ex and our daughter with my sexuality gave me a sense that my life was headed in the right direction.

Knowing that I was exhibiting true love and honor to my ex-boyfriend, by not sleeping with him and raising our child in the fear and admonition of the Lord gave me a new motivation and rededication to serve God wholeheartedly. Though not easy, this discussion with God caused me to pursue freedom from sexual bondage through relationship and fellowship with God with everything that I had.

The Perfect Excuse

Are you like I was before my emotional encounter with God? Do you have the perfect excuse as to why you are having sex outside of marriage as I did? Maybe you feel that the bond and feeling that's experienced while having sex is so pleasing that you can't imagine life without it. Maybe, you have never known that sex outside of marriage is wrong and hinders God's best in your life. Maybe, you've bought into the falsehood that fornication is okay because God knows your weakness and understands your need for sex. Whatever your reasoning is for practicing sex outside of marriage, I want you to know that I have been where you are. I understand your struggle and I want to help you the way that God helped me to become free.

Though I made many mistakes along the way, through much prayer and time spent with God I have discovered that there have been 7 basic secrets that I was able to use to assist in my quest to overcome the lust of my flesh. In the following chapters we will explore each of these secrets. See Table 2 on the following page, *The 7-Secrets of Celibacy Snap Shot.*

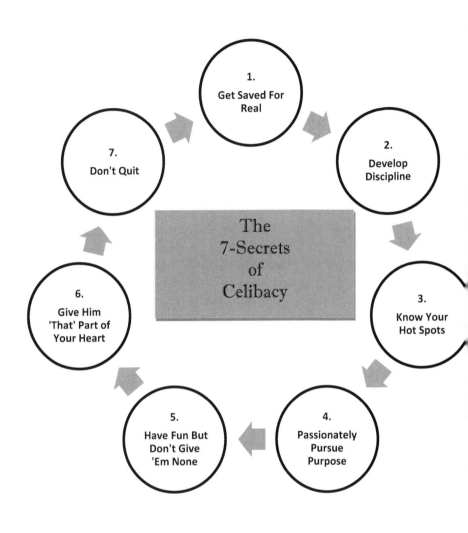

Table 2: The 7-Secrets of Celibacy Snap Shot

2

The

7-Secrets

Of

Celibacy

SECRET
#1

Get Saved

For Real

Make Jesus The Lord Over Your Life

My church, New Covenant Christian Center, under the leadership of Drs. Ron and Georgette Frierson (affectionately known as Lady G) spends a significant amount of time training our members in the art of lifestyle evangelism *(living a victorious life in Christ in such a way that our very existence would attract any type of sinner to the body of Christ)*. Along with other events staged throughout the year, during the spring/summer/fall months the ministry hosts a monthly evangelism effort where our entire body has the opportunity to go out and fulfill the great commission of winning souls into the Kingdom of God *(Matthew 28:19)*. Teams made up of our Church membership go into the neighborhoods of our city, and offer the gospel message of Jesus Christ.

For me this is one of the most fulfilling events of the year. There is nothing like seeing burden's lifted and yokes destroyed by the power of God right before your eyes, as one is led to give their lives to our Lord and Savior Jesus Christ. During this time of outreach, as a way to break the ice between sometimes complete strangers, and to measure where our subjects are in their relationship with God, the trained members conduct a short prewritten survey with its prospects.

During the appraisal, one of the final questions posed to the potential convert is, "If you were to die today and Jesus asked you, "Why should I let you into my heaven, what would your response be?" After regaining the wind that is seemingly knocked out of them by this final yet direct inquiry, we get an assortment of responses like:

"Because I was baptized when I was 10 at xyz Baptist;"

"Because I am a good person and I treat everybody right;"

"Because I am God's child;"

"I don't go out, smoke, or cuss;"

"I attend church every Sunday."

And one of my favorites,

"I have worked in the ministry for x amount of years."

Saying And Believing

What really amazes me is that these are mostly people who have been attending church all of their lives. I don't say this in a judgmental or critical tone, it just astounds me how misinformed a lot of people are about something as important as their eternal destiny and what it takes to receive true Salvation. While there are a host of ideas on what it takes to be saved from consistent church attendance to practicing good moral behavior, Romans 10:9 gives us the **only** pre-requisite for true salvation. Verse nine states that one only need "confess with your mouth the Lord Jesus and believe in your heart that God raised Him from the dead, (then) you will be saved."

That's it! All it takes to be saved, for real is confession, or saying with your mouth that Jesus is Lord, and believing in your heart that God raised Him from the dead. According to this scripture you are saved.

The problem that some people have with this is that it is too simple (Living In The Empowerment Zone, 2000). They cannot wrap their heads around the fact that Salvation can be equated to the two easy steps of saying and believing. The Apostle Paul states that, "God hath chosen the foolish things of the world to confound the wise; and God hath chosen the weak things of the world to confound the things which are mighty," *(I Corinthians 1:27)*.

God's thoughts are not our thoughts and his ways are not our ways (Isaiah 55:8). If you have not received true salvation and are not saved for real, now is a good time to accept Jesus into your heart. Without God, we can do nothing, *(John 15:5)*, including overcoming sexual sin. Philippians 4:13 reminds us that we can do all things through Christ who strengthens us. Often times single believers don't overcome sexual sin because they try and stop without the help of Christ, their only strength.

Prayer Of Salvation

Your unsuccessful attempt to keep yourself sexually pure causes you to resort to the lie that there is no hope. In return, you continue in sexual sin, misappropriating the grace of God on something that God has given you victory over. Getting saved for real is the fundamental step to walking in the Secrets of Celibacy. It gets God involved in your situation and allows God to break the power that sexual sin has over you. If you are ready to take the first step to coming out of sexual sin by getting saved for real, repeat the simple prayer of salvation below:

"Father, in the name of Jesus, forgive me of my sins. I believe that Jesus died and rose again for my sin. I ask that Jesus come into my heart and be the Lord over my life. Fill me with the Holy Spirit with the evidence of speaking in other tongues. Thank you Lord for hearing my prayer, coming into my heart, and being Lord over my life. According to Your Word, I confess that I am saved! I am born again! I am a child of God! Thank you for covering me in the precious blood of Jesus, in Jesus' name I pray, amen.

If you said that confession, I want to say, *"Congratulations!"* You are now saved for real! Welcome into the family of God! For more scriptural references that covers the decision that you just made, please read: Romans 3:10, Acts 17:30, Romans 10:9-10, and Romans 10:13.

Reciting this prayer not only sets the foundation for you to stop sinning sexually, it also gives you assurance of eternal life.

When you stand before God on the Day of Judgment and He asks, "Why should I let you into my heaven?"

You can say with assurance, "Because I have accepted Jesus as my personal Lord and Savior, I believe in my heart and have confessed with my mouth that Jesus is Lord!"

You are now ready to put your Faith in action by becoming a "doer" of God's Word.

Become A Doer Of The Word

The responses that I mentioned earlier that people give for how they know they are saved during our evangelism outreach mission are not all together wrong answers for being saved, these answers are just not the sole requirement for salvation. Now that you are saved for real, you are ready to put your faith in action by becoming a doer of The Word. Doing The Word causes Christians to experience victory in their salvation. After accepting Jesus as your personal Savior, the next step to experience triumph in Your Salvation is by properly applying The Word to your life.

Have you ever seen Christians that are seemingly blessed in everything that they do? Every time you look up they are exclaiming how good God is or how He has blessed them. They are always smiling and no matter what they are going through they seem to maintain a positive attitude about the situation.

Then there is another group of Christians that we question if they really do know Christ or if they will even make it into heaven. They've recited the sinner's prayer and made Jesus the Lord over their lives but they still casually cheat, steal, lie, cuss, smoke, drink, gamble, and have sex as if Jesus is not coming back.

I know that no one is perfect and each one of us is a work in progress, but this second group doesn't seem to care how their sinful lives affect God, themselves, and those around them. They are pretty content with a mediocre life on earth and barely making it into heaven. If you take a closer look at these two types of Christians more than likely you will discover that what the first group has mastered that the second group has not is putting The Word into action. The first group of Christian is considered a doer of The Word. The second group is what The Bible calls hearers only *(James 1:22)*.

Maturing In Christ

During the first two years of salvation, I was a model Saint. When I made Jesus my personal Lord and Savior, I immediately began to put The Word into action by working in ministry. I sincerely searched for God with my whole heart. As the newness wore off and reality set in, I gradually returned to the error of my ways. I wasn't so much a person who gave into swearing and drinking, and I did very little hanging out. But when it came to sex, I thought that I had to have it.

What happened between the time that I made Jesus Lord over my life and walking out The Word of God was maturity, or a lack thereof. When we first get saved, it is as if God puts our problems on hold for a year or two until we are mature enough spiritually to handle them, His way. He allows us to sit under The Word for a while, glean from other established Saints, and like a new born baby who is totally dependent on his parents to carry him, feed him, and clothe him, life is good. But when he gets older the parent expects him to mature by walking on his own, feeding himself, and putting on his own clothes. This time is a very uncomfortable time for the baby turned toddler. He fights to return to the comfort of his baby stages while his parents stand their ground to help him to mature.

God parents believers the same way. He knows if He continues to allow us to remain in the Infancy stages of our Christianity we won't grow. He requires that we begin to put into practice what we have learned up to that point. Little by little God takes the problems that we had before salvation off of hold so that we can handle them, the way that He would. Like the little baby who wants to be carried and does not want to walk on his own, feed or clothe himself, we don't want to handle things God's way. It's almost as if we feel that it is easier to revert back to our old ways.

A lot of single Christians are stuck and have been stuck in sexual sin for so long because they refuse to transition from a baby to a toddler in their Christianity. We can't even talk about going from toddler to adolescent, adolescent to teenager, teenager to adulthood in our salvation because we are trapped at the infancy stage. Rather than develop the skills necessary to get out and stay out of sexual sin, we say things like, "It's too hard," or "I can't do it." Instead of walking during our toddler years of Christianity, we continue to crawl around in the lust of our flesh. This causes us to live in an underdeveloped, immature, and defeated life.

The primary cause for this stagnate state for the believer is developing a trust that what God has ahead for us (celibacy until marriage) is better than what we are familiar with (sexual sin). This is where singles must be renewed in the spirit of our minds, *(Ephesians 4:23*; and Trust God with all of our hearts, *(Proverbs 3:5-6)*. God knew that our conversion would not be an easy one at least not in your own strength, so he put in place some special tools to help us. These tools build up the muscle needed to grow from faith to faith and glory to glory in this area. The tool that God designed to transform single saints into His image and likeness, from sexual sin to celibacy, is discipline.

SECRET

#2

Develop

Discipline

The Recipe For Spiritual Discipline

There is a place, position, and posture in God that only discipline can afford us- Pearl

During a women's meeting, my First Lady and mentor Dr. Georgette or Lady G as we affectionately call her, gave her audience six disciplines that every Christian should follow to remain victorious in our Christian walk (Authentic Living: Life Accroding to God's Plan, 2013). Like any good recipe, adding our own ingredients always makes the recipe personal for the cook. I have added *meditation* and *forgiveness* to the mix to make the disciplines my own. As I listened intently to my mentor, I found that for the most part, I had been consistent in applying these standards and this was more than likely the reason I had been so successful in my victory over sexual sin.

These disciplines include:

1. Reading God's Word
2. Prayer
3. Fasting
4. Giving
5. Praise and Worship
6. Church Attendance
7. Meditation

8. Forgiveness

Truthfully when I first heard these directives, I felt sort of self-righteous. Kind of like the rich young ruler who thought he had it all together when Jesus told him what he needed to do to inherit eternal life. As Jesus began to run down his ethical check list, the immature leader pulled out his invisible pen and pad of morality and mentally checked each of the commandments off as Jesus uttered them:

- Do not commit adultery (check)
- Do not steal (check)
- Do not bear false witness (check)
- Do not defraud (check)
- Honor your father and mother (check)

I know that it is not written anywhere, but I imagine that as Jesus was getting ready to continue with the rest of the commandments the young ruler probably interrupted him to inform him that there was no need to name all ten guidelines, because he had all of them down pat *(Mark10:17-27)*. As Lady G named the disciplines needed to lead a successful Christian life, I sat with confidence, sort of like the rich young ruler as if I had arrived.

My delay in accepting the information from Lady G didn't last long. As the Lord began to deal with me about staying teachable, I remembered that I had not arrived and that as disciplined as I may be, there is always room for growth. This shift in my train of thought allowed me to see where I had not only been successful with the disciplines, but I was able to spot where I had erred in keeping the directives. I saw ways to improve in maintaining the discipline needed to be successful as a Christian, especially as it pertained to sexual purity.

I would like to encourage you as God encouraged me to remain teachable concerning the disciplines of a believer. Be honest with where you are as it pertains to each discipline and gaining victory over sexual sin. Finally, seek God for a custom fit plan for your life to overcome sexual immorality.

Speaking of a custom fit plan, I would like to digress for a moment to let you know that this chapter is the meat and potatoes of this whole book. The glue if you will. Up until now, I would like to think that I have held your hand through sharing with you my own experiences. During this portion of the book as some of my editor friends say it, you may feel as if I have left the room as I am teaching the key principles that have kept me on the road to celibacy. This is all by design. To keep you entertained in this chapter, I was going to interject more "cutsie" (a word I made up to mean delightful, charming or appealing) stories of my own testimony, when the Lord instructed me not to. Although I do use my testimony in this section, my main focus was to give you an opportunity to fellowship with God. I want to encourage you to spend time with Him and allow Him to give you a tailor made plan specific for you and your victory over sexual sin. If you are tempted to skip this chapter because you feel that I have left the room and gotten impersonal, don't worry, I will be back before you know it. This is where God wants you to begin to think how you can begin to implement the discipline needed for abstinence in your own life.

The Discipline Of Reading God's Word

Once we get saved for real, The Bible says our spirits become re-born *(John 3:3)*. The tripartite nature of our entire being is ready to function in concert with one another. We are spirits who have souls which make up our mind, will, and emotions and all of that is housed in our bodies. Our spirits are nourished from God's Word, our souls gets its necessary substance from our intellectual intake through resources such as education, and finally our flesh consumes anything appealing to our lower natures, including natural food and sex.

It's no wonder why whichever part of our being that we feed most is the part that will become dominant in our lives. The goal is to have our recreated spirits rule our lives. In order to develop our newborn spirits, we must feed on an adequate supply of God's Word daily.

When I speak of reading God's Word I am speaking of getting God's Word on the inside of us. With today's technology, there are so many avenues in which one can read and hear God's Word to get it on the inside of us. The Bible is now on CD. We can download audio versions of The Bible on E-readers such as Kindle, cellular phones, live pod-casts, and of course in the traditional book form of The Bible.

Reading God's Word must be constant, consistent, habitual, and intentional. Some of us rarely skip meals and we cannot afford to skip opportunities to get daily dosages of God's Word. I have a Bible app downloaded on my IPhone and IPad so that the first thing I do each morning is read my daily devotional. Because our spirits never sleep, I keep a CD player by my bed at night so that I can listen to sermons from my Pastor, First Lady, and other notable ministers of the gospel. Throughout the day while at work or home, I can be found listening to audio versions of the Bible, faith based music, or Christian radio. This helps to keep my flesh under and spirit man strengthened.

Jesus came out victorious when He was tempted in the desert because He was full of The Word of God *(Matthew 4:11).* When sexual temptation knocks at our door we can experience the same triumph, as we consistently feed on God's Word.

When I first began to overcome sexual sin, one of the things that hindered me and kept me away from God's Word and what keeps many single Christians from reading God's Word is its reflective nature. The Word of God is likened to a mirror *(James 1:23).* Nearly everyone knows that The Word of God clearly tells us to flee sexual immorality *(I Corinthians 6:18).* Oftentimes, how the Word says that we should be and who we actually are contradicts.

Because we are imperfect, yet striving for perfection or who God has called us to be, the enemy tries to use shame (caused by sin) as a ploy to keep us from reading God's Word. What he doesn't want us to realize is that when we continue to read God's Word, despite our current conditions or what we look like, the more we will begin to resemble the reflection of the Word. Rather than sticking with the Word and allowing it to convert our beings from shame and nakedness to honor and glory, we like Adam and Eve (after the fall in the garden) run from God's glory and covering that can only be discovered through getting His Word on the inside of us.

Don't be deceived into thinking that just because you don't measure up to God's word that you can never change. This is a trick of the enemy. Failure to read God's Word because of guilt and condemnation brought on by sexual sin causes us to miss out on the transforming power found in The Word of God. In Romans 12: 2, The Apostle Paul encourages the believer, "Do not conform to the pattern of this world, but be transformed by the renewing of your mind. Then you will be able to test and approve what God's will is-His good, pleasing and perfect will" (NIV).

If we don't know what God's Word says, we don't know who we are. If we don't know who we are, we don't know that we have the power and authority to live sexually pure. God's Word is God's language to the believer. When we don't get the Word on the inside of us, the promises of God are foreign to us and we cannot properly communicate with God through prayer. God's Word is vital in conquering sexual sin in our lives because it is the basis for the discipline of prayer.

The Discipline Of Prayer

When I learned that prayer was simply communicating with God via His Word, my relationship with God went to a whole other level. Single believers get into so much trouble because we don't seek God's wisdom in prayer. Another definition for prayer is consulting with God. It is in this constant, continual talk with God that we are able to see what's ahead (good or bad), and plan our lives accordingly. Wise people see trouble coming and get out of its way, but fools go straight to it and suffer for it *(Proverbs 22:3- ERV)*.

As singles, we must train our spirits to pray about everything, small and great, so that we are conditioned to seek God. When I first stopped having sex in 1996, I knew that I could not do it alone. I prayed ahead to God about everything that triggered me sexually:

- "God the cologne that dude is wearing turns me on. I don't know if I can take much more of his cologne while we are alone."

- "Daddy, he is on his way over to my house; and it's

late. I don't have the nerve to tell him that it's too late... I know if he makes a move, I'm going to give him some, and I'm gone like it." You said to make no provisions for my flesh. I need your help, in Jesus' name."

- "Father in the name of Jesus, when this man treats me like a lady, paying for stuff, opening doors, and saying nice things, it makes me feel like I love him. I know that your love waits, and is patient. This can't be love; it has to be lust... I need your help. I know that if I give him some, I will blow my witness to him and others. I don't want to make you look bad and I don't want to look bad either. Please help!"

All of these prayers have something in common. They are spoken. God's word says, "When you pray, say" *(Luke 11:22)*. I don't know that there is such a thing as a silent prayer. These prayers are honest. God desires truth in the inward parts *(Psalms 51:6)*. God can not heal if we are not real. Next, each prayer is sealed in The Word of God. When seeking God for a way out of sexual sin, His Word must have final say (even if it's not what our flesh wants).

The final and most important part of prayer that we often overlook is listening to God for an answer and doing what He says. It is said that there are always three voices speaking to us through our conscious: *God's voice* is always lined up with His word. *Our voice* will always be our reasoning or what we want and the *devil's voice* will always be contrary to God's Word.

During times of sexual temptation, God will tell us His Word, "Flee sexual immorality" *(I Corinthians 6:1)*. Our voice will reason, "But, I love Him or Her." The devil voice will say, "Gone get you some, you can repent later." The more time we spend getting God's Word on the inside of us, the keener and stronger our spirits become and we are able to obey God's voice.

Don't be surprised with how God answers your prayer. Resist the temptation to harden your heart when God begins to move on your behalf as you start praying the types of prayers that I mentioned previously. It is because of these prayers that I have had a date unable to become erect. Another date was unable to find keys so that we could leave to go to a destination to have sex. I have had an interest leave my house with a sudden illness in the heat of the moment all because I prayed these honest, sincere, and Word filled prayers. "God is no respecter of persons" *(Acts 10:34)*. What he did for me, He will do for anyone.

Some may feel offended by my raw and bold prayers to God. I don't know how some stay celibate but it has been my experience that it is through these types of prayers that God has kept me. Some may be concerned that I put myself in harm's way and

90

am putting God to a foolish test. Some might even argue that prayers like these are not effective. Each of these arguments is untrue. What the devil wants us to believe is that we can't pray prayers like these to God because for some reason they seem sacrilegious. He knows that if we pray these types of prayers to God, He will not only keep us from sexual sin but He will change our hearts against the sin altogether. Instead of working against the will of God for our lives, when we pray these types of prayers, our desires become God's desire.

As powerful as prayer may be, some of you will find that sex has become a strong hold in your lives. You may discover that no matter how much you read God's Word or how much you pray, that you still find it difficult to shake the desire to have sex. In these instances, desperate times call for desperate measures. The bible teaches that you will not be able to overcome some sin without the discipline of **prayer** and **fasting** *(Matthew 17:21)*. I have found that in order to truly live out a life of sexual freedom, that I would not only have to pray but fast my way to victory.

The Discipline Of Fasting

Fasting is the discipline of abstinence from food or some other object of our affection with the purpose to subdue our carnal nature and discipline our souls- mind, will, and emotions *(Psalms 69:10)*. This is so that we can better respond to the promptings and leadings of God in our lives. Fasting is a command of Jesus and not a mere suggestion. In Matthew 6:16-18, Jesus told the disciples how to conduct themselves **when** they fasted, not **if** they fasted. I am convinced that if we can change our appetite we can change our lives. Because fasting and sexual sin are both directly connected to the cravings of our carnal nature, I find that nothing better assists me with abstinence from sex the way that fasting does.

Fasting Is Fun!

Medically fasting food helps us to eliminate waste and toxins from the body. Likewise fasting nonfood items such as the television, telephone, social media, gossip, people, and or places, eliminates negative behavior from our lives. Then we are better able to zero in on and obey the plan of God for our lives. In short fasting sharpens our senses to the things of God. While fasting is torture to our flesh, it can be fun if we change our view point about it. When we think about the benefits of fasting which include being in the divine will of God for our lives and experiencing God's best, it can be fun.

How Long Should One Fast?

It is not a matter of how long we should fast but that we do fast to free ourselves from sexual sin. It's also important that we fast on a regular and continual basis to be effective. For the 20 plus years that I have been saved, my Church has gone on a liquid fast from 6 p.m. every Tuesday night until 6 p.m. the following Wednesday evening. During this time, I can honestly say that I can only remember a few instances where I did not conduct a weekly fast of some sort. Initially, I would fast food, while drinking only liquids. Over the years as the spiritual attacks on my life increased and I began to see how fasting worked in allowing me to hear God more clearly, obey more readily, and get answers to prayer more speedily, I began to diversify my fasts. I have fasted for as little as a couple of hours with no food to a partial 40-day Daniel fast that can be found in Daniel 1:15; 10:2-3.

Fasting Guidelines

D ue to the serious nature of a no food fast, when your fast includes the absence of food, it is always recommended that you consult your doctor, spiritual leaders, and God before you begin. Although I have never fasted specifically to abstain from sexual sin, I am 100% sure that living a disciplined and fasted life is the reason that I have been able to remain celibate for so long. I have fasted for reasons that range from:

- A closer walk with God.
- The salvation of loved ones.
- Spiritual break through.

- Provision for my daughter in college.
- Me and my daughter's future husband.
- The answer to stubborn unanswered prayers.

If you have never fasted there are some brief guidelines to follow to become effective in fasting that include:

1. Have a purpose for your fast.
2. Determine the length of your fast.
3. Spend time in God's Word during your fast.
4. Expect God to answer your prayer.
5. Don't harden your heart when God responds, *His Way*.

In this case, the purpose for your fast is to become free from sexual sin. Through prayer you should repent of fornication and ask God to accept your fast to become free from sexual sin. To determine the length of your fast- seek spiritual and medical advice and find out a safe yet adequate time frame for you. If you are just getting started, try fasting food for a couple of hours during a specific day of the week. You may want to fast during your lunch period from 12-3 p.m. each Monday for three months, for the purpose of effectively hearing the voice of God concerning His plan to free you from promiscuity. The length of the fast is not as important as actually fasting. As with any discipline, the more that you practice it, the more endurance you develop and will be able to fast for longer periods of time.

Spend time reading your Word during your times of fasting. This accelerates the training of your spirit to hear the voice of God, and develops in you an expectation for God to answer you with His perfect plan to become free of sexual sin once and for all. Remember God is not out to hurt you but to help you. He is all powerful, all knowing and everywhere at once. He knows just what it will take to free you from sexual sin. Once God begins to move on your behalf, which may include removing and replacing people, places, and things which causes you to sin sexually, don't respond immaturely by hardening your heart out of rebellion. Instead ask God to help you to accept His will and His way for your life, because He knows best. Offer your body as a living sacrifice, holy and acceptable which is your reasonable act of worship *(Romans 12:1)*.

The Discipline Of Giving

You may be wondering how on earth giving fits into living a life of celibacy. Outside of companionship, one of the key reasons I think singles fall into sexual sin is because we don't take God at His Word regarding how to overcome the financial pressures of this world. Rather than believing God to meet our needs, we have relied on a man or woman to take up the monetary slack in our lives. Some of us are so afraid of being without and alone that we compromise with sexual relationships to keep our heads above water fiscally. It's sad but so many singles are not only working one or two jobs to meet day to day needs, we are working three and four jobs just to pay the rent. This should not be.

God has outlined a way in His Word for us to have our every need met. However, we must participate in His giving principle to see it at work in our lives. We have to rid ourselves of the world's mindset that says we have to have a sugar daddy or sugar momma in order to get ahead in life. No matter the type of giving, the discipline of giving positions us to get God's best in our lives.

Types Of Giving

The two major types of giving are:

> 1. Tithe- unlike the other types of giving, the tithe is **NOT** optional. This type of donation is **required** by all believers to give God (through local church membership) dues of one tenth of all of our increase. For example, if we work and get a pay

check for $2,200.00 per week, our tithe would be $220 ($2,200 x 10%). The benefit of the tithe is that it rebukes the devourer on our behalf and sets the foundation for God to meet our **EVERY** financial need. Some feel that they cannot afford to tithe. As a believer it is my experience that I can't afford not to tithe *(Malachi 3:8-10).*

2. Offering- The tithe ensures the window of heaven blessing on our lives and offerings into special things such as missions, building fund projects, and love offerings into the lives of our man and/or woman of God, determines the speed of flow in that window *(Luke 6:38).*

I know a lot of Christians (men and women) who give in to sexual sin to have their financial needs met. They stay in bad relationships because they have not mastered the concepts of tithing and giving. One young lady that I know says that she stayed in a bad relationship for over 17 years because she thought that she needed the money, despite how hard God and others tried to tell her otherwise.

Although I can't say that I have ever stayed in a relationship because of money, I can say that because I learned that my maker is my husband (spouse) *(Isaiah 54:5),* I am more able to take God at His Word when it comes to meeting my need. No matter what

97

things look like God has never allowed me or my daughter to go without the things we want and need. One time while working at a bank, I had a really financially wealthy man ask me out on a date. I knew he was not a Christian because every other word that came out of His mouth was a curse word. He knew that I was saved. As I look back, I can't believe the boldness that I had, when I told him, "I don't date unsaved men." He was very upset by my response but allowed me to finish his business. Before I completed his transaction I removed myself from his presence to go into the company's board room to talk with God about his proposition.

"God, you know this man has a lot of money and he's not saved. Why would you allow him to ask me out? You know I like money."

God responded, "You're the one tripping about money. The man that I have for you will have money. Money is no big deal to me."

At the conclusion of our board meeting, I walked away with a new found assurance in God's Word. I knew that He didn't want me to hook up with the wrong man for the wrong reason. From that point on I have been able to date men by looking at their hearts and not their pockets. Through the process of taking all of my wants and needs to God in prayer and watching Him exceed them, I have experienced that my maker truly is my husband *(Isaiah 54:5)*. Any good husband would not allow his wife to go around prostituting herself to have her needs meet.

God will not allow a man or woman to out give him in our lives, if we are faithful in giving of tithes and offering. I encourage you if you are not a tither and a giver, to begin to give. Start out paying your tithe. When needs and desires arise, take pressure off of yourself and put it on The Word of God. Using the vehicle of prayer, refuse to return to a sexual relationship to have your needs met. God promises to supply all of your need according to His riches in Glory through Christ Jesus *(Philippians 4:19)*. God is not a man that He should lie, nor the son of man that He should repent *(Numbers 23:19)*. He promises that if you delight yourself in Him, that He will give you the desires of your heart *(Psalms 37:4)*.

Now don't get me wrong, I believe that it's okay in a committed relationship that is leading to marriage, for two people to help each other out financially and otherwise, but this should not be used as a scheme to hang over someone's head to have sex or keep them in a wrong relationship. God promises the believer that if we pay our tithes and give offerings that He would open up the window of heaven for us and pour out a blessing that we would not have room enough to receive *(Malachi 3:8-10)*. This truth dispels the myth that we must stay in wrong relationships in order to have our material needs met.

Since I have been tithing and giving of offerings, I've watched God keep His Word in my life. Although I have what is considered a good job with benefits according to the world's standards, nearly 20 years of tithing and giving has allowed me to live on the salary of a **sower** and not simply off of the salary of my

employer. The salary of a sower does not allow me to live life fiscally irresponsible. Rather, it allows me to tap into an unlimited reservoir of God's provision and favor for me and my daughter's life.

I have been able to not only meet my day to day needs on the salary of a sower, I have been blessed to take nice vacations, build a new home (after being homeless for several years), drive a luxury car, send my daughter to college, and live at peace financially. It also does not mean that I have not had trying times financially, but when those times occur, I am at peace because my maker is my husband. When I have a need I let Him supply all of my need according to His riches in glory by Christ Jesus *(Philippians 4:19)*. Not only does God supply my need He does exceedingly, abundantly, above all that I could ask, think, or imagine *(Ephesians 3:20)*

Once I am obedient in exercising God's promise in paying my tithes and offerings and have freed myself from giving of my body in wrong relationships due to financial pressures, I am free to give God something more precious, more intimate, and more personal. I am free to give of myself freely and entirely in praise and worship.

The Discipline Of Praise And Worship

When being weaned from the lust of the flesh nothing temporarily pacifies and eventually eradicates our urge for sexual pleasure the way that praise and worship does. It is in praise and worship that we offer our entire beings to God as living sacrifices, which is our reasonable service *(Romans 12:1)*. We praise God for what He has done and worship Him for who He is. Praise and worship is a humbling and intimate experience where we are forced spiritually and mentally to take our eyes off of ourselves and having sex and placing them on the one true, and living God. Praise and worship involves us lifting our hands, opening our mouths and surrendering all to God.

Praise and worship is a lot like sex in that we are giving the most intimate part of ourselves to the object of our affection. We worship God by adoring Him. We thank Him for being our Lord and savior, for loving us enough to die for us and delivering us from sexual immorality (even if we don't see the manifestation of our deliverance). We thank God for being our life, our love, and the name above all names. These words and acts of love toward God draws us closer to God and Him to us while moving us further away from sexual sin. When we worship God we can do so by kneeling, standing, sitting, or lying prostrate in surrender to Him.

Just as we would become naked, unashamed, and without pretense during sexual intimacy, we give ourselves to God when we go to Him honestly, without condemnation and we are real about

101

where we are sexually. When we are consistent, over time, worship takes the fragments of our souls caused by sexual sin and gathers it back to its original state. This is why the enemy works over time to get us to live in guilt and condemnation because he knows if we go past praise into worship, we are out of his reach and we can become free from sexual sin. Praise and Worship replaces the vulnerability, closeness and intimacy we share with another while having sex and our affection is directed solely toward God.

The Discipline Of Committed Fellowship In Church

When struggling with sexual sin, our church attendance is usually the first thing that wanes. It's easy to adopt an attitude of being the only one that is experiencing a hardship. We feel that church people are looking at us in a judgmental and critical way and that they just don't understand. These feelings of accusation keep us from the strength developed from others during consistent church attendance.

We are not to forsake ourselves with the assembling together of the saints *(Hebrews 10:25)*. When I was drowning in the guilt of sexual sin, I knew that the temptation to have sex was so strong that it was impossible for me to free myself. I somehow knew that I needed to experience the love and truth that came from God through other believers, during my time of struggle. It did not matter that I may have just had an all-night sexual rendezvous the night before, maybe got some (sex) right before I came to church service, or if I intended on having sex after church ended. I cannot tell you the number of times that I have been unknowingly supported not to have sex just by going to church.

Rather it was an usher on the door who met me with his regular and uplifting greeting, "Hey Kangs Kid" (slang for Kings Kid), an elder in the ministry waiting with open arms to extend a hug, or a lay person offering a simple smile of acceptance. It was church attendance that gave me the muscle and desire to stop having sex. Like a lot of singles who are involved in sexual sin, I originally thought these people were being secretly judgmental when I saw them, because I couldn't imagine why someone could be so nice to someone who was in sin. Then I grasped the fact that nine times out of ten these people didn't know or care what I had been doing the night before. I began to understand that people had their own problems. I realized that other church members were just genuinely happy to extend the grace of God to someone else, just as they had received it.

I think social media, the electronic church, and tele-evangelism are great advancements in technology. They are awesome tools that are used to reach those who cannot attend church due to unforeseen circumstances such as hospitalization, near death experiences, being on vacation, and other occasions where church attendance is impossible. However, it should not be used to replace consistent and regular church attendance.

When we are caught in sexual sin, no accountability breeds irresponsibility. Missing church puts no pressure on our flesh to stop living in sin. Something happened over time when I was consistently present at church. Faith comes by hearing and hearing by The Word of God *(Romans 10:17)*. The more that I heard encouraging words from the saints and pastor's sermons, the more I was able to believe that what the Word of God said about me was true. This provided me with the confidence needed to come out of sexual sin.

Instead of being offended by the accountability that church attendance afforded me, over time I welcomed it. In fact, knowing that the church had an expectation that its members would live, not perfect but right, made me think twice before committing sexual sin. Church attendance also brought about resilience in my spirit. Ecclesiastes 4:12 says that a threefold cord is not easily broken. The saying that there is strength in numbers is true. Coming out of isolation and joining other likeminded Christians in regular church attendance has a strengthening power that assisted me in overcoming sexual sin.

The Discipline Of Meditation

What we allow to go on in our head is what we will allow to go on in our lives. Anything that we think about long enough we will eventually act upon. God's Word tells us to be renewed in the Spirit of our minds (Ephesians 4:23). Replacing old thoughts of the comfort, false security, or sheer bliss we felt during times of illicit sex with God's Word is crucial when it comes to staying out of sexual immorality.

When I meditate God's Word, I am in essence, thinking about and musing over in my mind, The Word of God concerning a particular situation. Over the years, I have realized that I am more prone to be tempted sexually during two times of the day:

1. Early in the morning (times when I would get what is called a "quickie" – sex that requires little if any foreplay and lasts about 10 to 15 minutes).
2. At night- a time where sex was a little more in depth because there was time to prepare for the event and there were no distractions.

During these times, I found that my mind had the capacity to go wild with thoughts of how things used to be sexually. These are moments that I could not afford to lie in lust. I could not afford to lie in bed or wherever I was during these times and have sexual fantasies. I had to combat these thoughts by meditating on The Word of God.

A lot of scripture isn't necessary when meditating. In fact, it only takes one. My favorite verse to think on during times of sexual temptation is I Corinthians 6:18, "Flee Sexual Immorality."

When my mind is bombarded with visuals of sex, I begin to speak with my mouth,

"I flee sexually immorality."

Because the thoughts don't usually go away right away, I am consistent; continuing to speak:

"I flee sexual immorality."

During your times of meditation take heart if the thoughts of sex seem to continue to resurface in your mind. Don't be concerned about repeating or quoting the same scripture over and over because it feels funny, rehearsed, or as if nothing is changing. Just continue to quote the scripture to yourself, until like antibiotics does a cold, the negative thoughts break. To solidify my words, I think about what I am speaking. I imagine myself not only fleeing or running from sexual sin, but I see myself away from the situation all together. I shift my mind to refocus on the results that fleeing from sexual immorality brings. I think about my wedding day where I am standing at the altar ready to marry the man of my dreams. I imagine myself having a good conscience before God, my soon-to-be husband, and witnesses. All because I will know that I did not give into sexual temptation, having waited on God to bring my mate. I may even envision myself talking to my daughter Jai or other young and mature women alike about how I waited on God. I picture how encouraged they would be because they would feel that if God could help me to hold out; He would also provide a way of escape from sexual sin for them as well.

For those of you who think that meditation is wasteful day dreaming, I encourage you to read the story of Jacob who changed an entire breed of cattle through the art of meditation *(Genesis 30:25-43)*. Joshua 1:8 encourages the believer to meditate The Word day and night in order to have good success. If meditation can work for animals, how much more can it be effective for those overcoming sexual sin? Meditation in a nutshell is replacing defeated thoughts of sexual sin with thoughts of sexual purity. It only requires that you quote one scripture continuously, see yourself acting on that verse and it won't be long before you are experiencing victory over fornication.

The Discipline Of Forgiveness

Forgiveness is coming to a place in my heart where I stop blaming and feeling resentment towards self and others for wrongs done. Most believers have no problem with forgiving others for trespasses committed against them, but when it comes to forgiving themselves, they find it nearly impossible. When we don't forgive ourselves for our sexual transgressions, God can't forgive us *(Matthew 6:15)*.

If we wallow in guilt and condemnation, we remain stuck in our offenses and are not able to come boldly before the throne of grace to receive help and deliverance from sexual sin in our time of need *(Hebrews 4:16)*. We must also remember that "There is no condemnation for those who are in Christ Jesus" *(Romans 8:1)*. I have had to keep these two truths in mind on many occasions in

107

order to partake in the freedom, liberty, and grace of God needed to move me from sexual sin to sexual purity.

On one particular occasion, my daughter Jai was about two years old. I laid in bed heavy burdened with the guilt and condemnation caused by the sexual sin in my life. In an attempt to relieve myself of the shame, I looked into Jai's eyes and said something like,

"Mommy loves you."

As quick as I uttered the Words out of my mouth Jai responded back to me,

"Your love stinks!"

"What did you say?" I retorted in unbelief.

"Your love stinks," my two year old commented matter-of-factly.

After sitting up and asking her to repeat herself several times, I realized that she was saying what I thought she was saying. Talk about condemnation. I felt so ashamed. Feeling bad about my sin alone would not change my situation though. I knew that I needed to take action by asking God for His help.

When we commit fornication, condemnation or sinners remorse is one of the first emotions that show up on the scene after the act. What we fail to realize is that guilt, condemnation or sinner's remorse alone does little if anything to move us from our transgressions toward the deliverance that we so desire. Instead of sinner's remorse, what we need is true repentance. Sinner's remorse causes us to feel bad about our sexual sin for a brief moment until the temptation presents itself again, creating a 360 degree effect. We turn from the sin only to revisit it again, at an opportune time. True repentance however, produces a 180 degree outcome. We call God on the scene by petitioning His help in the matter through prayer. Where sinner's remorse keeps us locked in and looking at the wrongs we've committed, true repentance focuses us on God and His viable solutions.

Although, initially I felt an enormous amount of guilt and shame from my daughter's response, instead of wallowing in my woes, I asked God for forgiveness and help in being an example to my daughter and others that we all could be proud of. I then went about practicing the other disciplines outlined in this chapter to prepare my spirit to stay out of sexual sin. Finally, I refused to allow myself, others, or the devil to feed me thoughts of guilt by revisiting my sinful past.

Forgiving ourselves and others does not mean we deny the truth. Neither does it mean that we do not need to make amends when we have done wrong to ourselves and others. There have been instances because I was a Christian who knew better and my ex-boyfriend was not as mature in his walk with God that I have had to apologize for not being a good example of Christ to him. I did not do this in my own strength and I want to encourage you to be sure that you are not trying to make amends in your own power either.

It is imperative that while you are seeking to make reparation with God, yourself, and others that you seek the help of

God via prayer before you do this. This will prevent you from falling back into sexual sin with that person again, having to repent for the same sin. Repentance without change yields an unrepentant heart. After a while, the person does not take you seriously and your actions are no longer considered repenting as you are now repeating the cycle of sin without change.

Be mindful that Jesus took all of our sins upon Himself when He was nailed to the cross. He gave us victory over sin, when He arose from the dead. Asking others for forgiveness not only holds us accountable from repeating the sin but it also clears our hands of innocent blood when we have caused others to stumble in sin. As you may already know, forgiving ourselves of sin is not always easy, but it is necessary. Forgiveness provides us the freedom that is needed to partner with God on His personal plan for our deliverance over the lust of our flesh.

Beware Of The Deception Of Discipline

One would not expect a new born baby to have the ability to bench press a 100 pound weight. Likewise, you cannot expect a new born Christian or an aged old Christian with an underdeveloped spirit to overcome sexual sin without properly building a muscle of resistance to tear down the stronghold of lust in their lives. The eight disciplines of a believer are designed to help single believers to exercise their spirits in preparation to overcome sexual sin.

I want to warn you to beware of the deception of discipline. After you have practiced the disciplines mapped out in this chapter, you will begin to experience victory over sexual sin as well as victory over other areas of your life. There will come a time where you may feel like a well-oiled machine that is working on every cylinder. You begin to feel a confidence in yourself that you haven't felt in a long time or may have never felt. This is a time where you may be tempted to slack off on your disciplines.... DON'T! "The way you start with God, is the way you stay with God" (Frierson G. , 2014). Your adversary the devil is prowling around seeking someone to devour *(I Peter 5:8)*. The enemy of your faith will leave for a season only to return at what he feels is an opportune time, hoping to find you slipping in these disciplines *(Luke 4:13)*.

While I don't want to overwhelm you with a bunch of does and don'ts of a believer, I want to encourage you to work each of these disciplines into your daily lives until over time they become automatic. We are encouraged to come to God as little children *(Luke 18:16-17)*. We should always approach the disciplines of the believer as teachable children of God knowing that we can always learn from them. Once we have properly mastered them we are ready to apply the disciplines in keeping us out of sexual sin. We can employ the disciplines to not only help us in understanding what triggers us sexually, but use them as a tool to steer clear of sex all together, as we get to know and stay away from our sexual Hot Spots.

SECRET
#3

Know
Your Hot Spots

Knowing our hot spots requires becoming aware through the careful study of one's sexual history what stimulates us to have sex outside of marriage, and then staying away from these danger zones. I wish I could say that I have been celibate for nearly two decades because I'm never tempted or that I am so saved for real that I don't or haven't put myself in situations that would stir up my desire for sex. While I don't *intentionally* put myself in places to be tempted sexually, as I mentioned in the discipline of prayer, I have found myself in a number of situations where if it were not for the grace of God, I would not have a testimony of abstinence.

When thinking of a sexual hot spot one may think of it as a place on our body that turns us on sexually when touched (for those of us who have been sexually active). While this may be considered a hot spot, when discussing The 7-Secrets of Celibacy, knowing our hot spot goes beyond physical touch. In fact, our hot spot could be a person, place, thing, situation, sight, or even a smell. Our hot spot is anything or anyone that stimulates or triggers us sexually.

After God began to deal with me about ending sexual sin and I got an understanding of how much having sex outside of marriage really hurt God and limited His best for my life, I began to seek God for his help. I not only wanted to know how not to stop having sex, I sought out ways that prevented me from being placed in compromising situations. God caused me to revisit my sexual history and find out the reason I began to have sex, what aroused me sexually, and when and where I was more apt to be tempted sexually. I had to become a master investigator of my sexual past.

Fatherlessness

What I discovered would not only help me to become free sexually, but it also showed me how to unmask myself and be real with God, myself, and others, especially the men that I have dated. Through some time spent in prayer and exercising the other disciplines found in Secret #2, I found out that the primary reason that I began to have sex was due to fatherlessness. Keep in mind that I have always known who my Father is and we have always had a great, although distant relationship. Because he was not present in my home, I have always had an unquenchable, indescribable desire to fill the void that his absence caused. My unsuccessful attempts to fill the "daddy void" in my heart caused me to read love from a man differently than how God had intended it. Instead of defining love from I Corinthians 13, I gauged how much a man loved me by how well he filled what I termed as my *four T's of love.* The four T's of love include: touch, talk, treasure, and time.

Because my Dad was not actively involved in a huge portion of my child hood, I was emotionally deficient when it came to the nurture that a dad offers his daughter. Things like basic touch from a daddy's hug to allay his daughters fear from a bad dream. Simple conversations about how my day went. Financial support for things as small as milk money for school was lacking. Also, the absence of time spent in such normal things as a bed time story left me hungry for the attention of my daddy.

Seeking The Attention Of A Man

God caused me to realize that at an early age this lack of genuine love from my Dad sent me seeking the attention of a man. As a child, I would innocently go out of my way to please any man in my life. This left me open for abuse, both physical and emotional. Because relationships with a man were somewhat foreign to me, I fumbled my way around trying to figure out what it took to please a man. Because I was taken advantage of by some adult men in my life, I developed the false notion that the only way a woman could please a man was in the bed.

Due to sexual abuse, I did not know how to tell men no to sexual advances. I was always stuck in that little girl's body who just wanted to please her daddy. Although I didn't want to please my daddy sexually, I found that all my male relationships were mirrored by my relationship with my dad. The fact that I lacked the innocent touch of my Dad set in motion the thought that when a man touched me, even if it was an abusive slap or unwanted fondling, I mistook his touch as love. Because I did not spend a whole lot of day to day time with my dad, when a man spent time

116

with me and talked to me even though it may have been inappropriate, I confused his time and talk with me as love. Because my Dad gave very little financial support for me as a child, I found that when a man spent his treasure or money on me, I was in love. It didn't matter that he may have been trying to manipulate me in the relationship. What I termed as, "The Four T's of Love" I found, had become my hotspots.

God Can't Heal If You're Not Real

As embarrassing and painful as my new found revelation was to face, it was one of the most freeing discoveries that I have ever found out about myself. Anytime I found myself in a relationship, I would use my new discovery as talking points to God in prayer. God desires truth in the inward part *(Psalms 51:6)*. One time while attempting to hide my feelings about a relationship from myself, God and others, God spoke to my spirit that,

"I can't heal if you're not real."

What God was saying is if I wanted to be truly set free from sexual sin, I was going to have to be honest with myself, God, and, others about my "hot spots." This realization set me totally free. I began to just be real with God. If I went out on a date and something as small as the hand holding was too much for me, I would tell God, "God I felt a little hot in the butt holding dude's hand, what should I do?"

117

I continued to remind God of His Word, "God, you said to make no provision for the flesh. You said you wouldn't put anything on me that I couldn't bear." I even told God that I felt like a wimp if I told the guy how I was feeling.

Each time God made a way of escape *(I Corinthian 10:13)*. Sometimes he would change the natural order of things and perform a miracle. I have literally been in positions where I was so hot and bothered that my salvation meant nothing, my witness meant nothing, and God and His Word meant nothing. At the moment, I just wanted to have mad, passionate sex. It was because I said these prayers to God prior to and during hot and steamy circumstances, that God performed what I call my "Sea Splitting Experiences." Because, like God did for Moses and the children of Israel when their backs were up against the wall, He performed a miracle to save them by splitting the Red Sea. In the instances that I previously discussed in the Discipline of Prayer where my date was unable to become erect, the guy lost his keys so that we couldn't go to a planned location to have sex, and an interest left my home abruptly after things became hot and heavy because he suddenly became ill, were all "Sea Splitting Experiences."

Naturally I wanted to be mad at God, because I couldn't fulfill the lusts of my flesh and have sex. Fortunately for me, I quickly realized that this was God's sovereign protection on my life. I decided that this was not the time to harden my heart as God had answered my prayer, HIS way, *(Hebrews 3:15)*. Finally, I recognized that God was not trying to keep something from me; He was trying to shield me and the other person from breaking our covenant with Him.

God would sometimes answer my prayer by encouraging me to talk to my boyfriend at the time and let him know how I was feeling. To let him know, "Hey, I feel as if we are getting a little too touchy feely," or "I think we need to do some outings in the day time where we are not so tempted to have sex."

For the most part my date was usually very receptive and accommodated my requests. There have been a few occasions where this discussion seemed to turn some men on and they wanted to see how far they could push the envelope. I knew in these instances that he was not the man for me and eventually, I would call off the relationship.

The Cause Of Compromise

In addition to the four T's of love, I found that another one of my hotspots was my likelihood to compromise sexually when I felt as if I was losing the relationship. Going back to my childhood and living without my Father, I found that I would do just about anything to see or be around my Daddy. When my dad called and told me he was coming to get me, I was elated. If something came up and this didn't happen, I would be devastated for days. I became depressed and moped around all day. I began to internalize his absence as rejection and thought if I was only good enough or pretty enough then my dad would be in my life more. This carried over into my relationships with men in that albeit real or imaginative, I found myself putting up with more than I should with a man because I didn't want to lose him.

Even after I stopped having sex, when I felt as if I was in love with a man and I began to feel threatened by conflict in the relationship, I found myself less likely to challenge him with The Word. I became more docile, not for the simple purpose of keeping the peace, but I feared losing the relationship, like I feared not seeing my daddy as a little girl. Instead of voicing what it was that I wanted and needed from the relationship, I was more apt to go with the flow and not disrupt the order of things. Even if things were not right and I was uncomfortable about a situation.

The problem that this posed was a man not sensitive to the voice of God, overly concerned about his own needs, and/or not in tune with who I was or what I needed in the relationship, could take advantage of me. This left me in a vulnerable and compromising position both sexually and emotionally. Instead of being hurt and hurting God, I ran from the relationship.

While this secret is no more important than the others, it is the most practical and often the most ignored of the 7-Secrets of Celibacy. Romans 13:14 encourages the believer, *"to put on the Lord Jesus and make no provision for the flesh, to fulfill its lusts."* It was Shakespeare in the play Hamlet who said, "To thine own self be true" (Shakespeare, 2001). Knowing your hot spot is where the single saint has to exercise being honest with God, self, and others and allow God to bring him/her out of sexual sin causing them to be free to Passionately Pursue Purpose.

SECRET #4

Passionately Pursue Purpose

"Please Pray for Me, I Want To Have Sex!"

"Loneliness is not a lack of people in our lives, but a lack of purpose" (Trimm, 2011).

Purpose focuses us toward destiny and distracts us from the pitfalls of sexual sin. If it is said that idle hands are the devils workshop, an idle mind his play ground, then it is also safe to say that a single life without purpose is doomed to fall into sexual sin.

It was not too long after I celebrated 17 years of sex free living, that I was literally dumbfounded when I was caught off guard by a strong urge to have sex. The lustful longing shocked me to the point that I had to call for back up. I sent a text to my mentor, Lady G to solicit her prayers in the matter (something I almost never do). The text read something like,

"Please pray for me, I want to have sex!" (It would be funny if it were not so serious).

After she addressed the situation, reminding me that I was being attacked by the devil and told me to tell my flesh to shut up and speak The Word over my life, her next question really caused me to think. She asked me something like,

"You've never been attacked in *that* area of your life before?"

That is when it dawned on me that yes, I had been previously tempted to have sex, but probably not within the last 10 years (at least)! This thought baffled me even more than the craving for sex that I had just experienced. I began to wonder, how did that happen? How does one who has been sexually active in the past and who enjoyed having sex, as I did, not have urges for intercourse for over ten years? And how or when did I open the door for sexual temptation to re-enter my life.

Purpose Keeps Us On Course

During my brief internal audit is when it hit me, that up until this point, I had been so busy living out my God given destiny that I had not had time to even think about no less battle against the temptation to have sex. I had been doing what many people only dream of. I had found and been passionately pursuing purpose. Purpose has in it the power to keep us on course, focused, and reduces the temptation to sin sexually. Purpose takes a seemingly mundane, daunting task and makes it fun and adventurous. Purpose gives us a love for life. You've heard that time flies when we're having fun? I like to say that time flies when we're passionately pursuing purpose.

It is because of a passionate pursuit of purpose that Jacob was able to work seven years for his beloved Rachel's hand in marriage as if it were only a few days *(Gen 29:20)*. After being swindled by her deceptive father into marrying his oldest daughter Leah, Jacob worked an additional seven years for the hand of his adored fiancé, because he knew that marrying Rachel was a part of his life's purpose, *(Genesis 29:27)*.

124

I have discovered through the teaching at New Covenant Christian Center Church that all human purpose involves glorifying God and benefiting others outside of oneself. We glorify God when we get saved for real. This is the initial step needed to fulfill our destiny. Everything else regarding purpose involves us glorifying God by being a benefit to others.

The Primary Benefactors To Our Pursuit Of Purpose

Since the latter part of purpose involves benefiting others, our children and or family should be the first recipient of our passionate pursuit. Prior to getting saved for real, I had an overwhelming sense of how the consequences of my actions affected my daughter, Jai (good or bad). I believed in the law of what some call karma but what The Bible calls sowing and reaping *(Galatians 6:7)*. I knew that everything that I did, my child would become a carbon copy. I knew that if I came home at all times of the night, drank, smoked, cussed and had sex outside of marriage that one day she would too. I also knew that all the things that I had already done prior to getting saved for real could possibly affect her life. So many single Christian men and women think that just because we do things out of our kid's sights, that our kids will not be affected. This could not be further from the truth.

While we may be able to keep things from people, the eyes of the Lord are in every place *(Proverbs 15:3)*. What we do in the dark will come to the light *(I Corinthians 4:5)*, even if it manifested through our children. The very thought of this terrified me and caused me to embrace my purpose of parenting and benefiting others with everything that I had.

Just as I knew that my bad choices would influence Jai, I also knew that I could begin to change the face of my future and hers by changing my way of life. I enrolled in college, got a job to support us, and I joined and began to volunteer in a faith filled ministry. These things replaced negative premarital sexual behavior with positive activities. Gradually, I began to see myself differently. My daughter never had to become a victim of my lascivious lifestyle, and others who knew me witnessed my productive transformation as well. My family and friends became the primary benefactors to my pursuit of purpose. (Please note that our family and friends have the power of choice. Even when we live uprightly before them, they still may choose to live in sin. Our responsibility is not to determine their response to our passionate pursuit of purpose. Our job is to walk blameless before them as to be an example).

Where I once hung out every day of the week, I was now in church three to five times a week or at home helping my daughter with her homework. Eventually, I got my finances in order, graduated from college, bought a house, became independent of state aid and things began to look up for my daughter and I. My life was so full of new and positive activities that I literally did not have time to think about or partake in my old destructive ways. Over time everything that I had ever asked God for had manifested in my life, above and beyond what I could ask or think *(Ephesians 3:20).*

The problem that I had was I had reached all of my goals and my life hit a plateau. I became comfortable and somewhat stagnate in pursuing purpose, failing to reach for new heights in life. Since my life had changed for the better so drastically, I thought that all of my reason for being had been fulfilled. I didn't realize that God had new heights for me to conquer and that I needed to be cautious of comfort while pursuing purpose.

By the time Jai was getting ready to go to college, God began to put new and innovative ideas in my spirit. During Jai's sophomore year of high school, God told me to start my own publishing company. He told me that I would write and publish my own work and conduct speaking engagements. Because I did not know anyone else who had started their own publishing company and I did not want to do the work needed to start a new business, I rejected the idea.

I had decided that I would live in the safe place of least resistance by working a nine-to- five-job for the rest of my life, retiring, and as my Pastor often says, "Study war no more." The period of excitement that I had from completing graduate school, buying a new home, getting out of debt, purchasing a new vehicle and starting a new career had worn off. Where victories once

127

seemed to flood my life, they now had become a faint memory. When things began to digress for me professionally and personally (as I had received at least two significant pay cuts on my job within two years in the midst of sowing considerably in the giving of my tithes and offerings), I was forced to revisit God's initial plan of purpose and start a publishing company.

My Belly Of The Whale Experience

In addition, while there is absolutely nothing wrong with wanting to get married, I noticed that I became overly concerned with the notion. Instead of trusting God to send me my mate, I had taken matters into my own hands. To the naked eye, no one could tell, but in my spirit I had become anxious to become wed. For the first time in my saved life, I felt as if I was beginning to settle for less than God's best in every area of life. There was something missing. I had lacked the passion to pursue purpose. I call this period of my life my "Belly of the Whale Experience" *(Jonah 1-3)*. I, like Jonah was in a self-inflicted stinky place, all because I refused to obey God in pursuing purpose by starting a publishing company. As I began to seek God about the next phase for my life, something amazing happened. I regained sight of my purpose. I rediscovered the fact that I was to live my Christian life in such a way that people would see it and want to know the God that I serve.

Through this endeavor to resuscitate purpose in my life, I have discovered that most saved saints fall into sexual temptation because instead of climbing to new levels in purpose we embrace the thief of our destiny, comfort. We allow God to do so many amazing things in our lives that we cannot imagine that He could possibly have more in store for our lives. Instead of maturing in purpose, we get sidetracked, distracted, and off course. If we are not careful, we risk over a process of time, becoming okay with being okay. We adopt the world's definition of purpose for our lives by staying on jobs longer than we should, cultivating relationships that we have long outgrown, and putting up with circumstances that God has given us the authority to overcome. Finding Mr. or Mrs. Right and remaining status quo seems to become our only goal in life.

God Always Wants Us To Do More

No matter how young or old we are, no matter how successful we have become, or how many goals we have attained, God wants us to do more. This may come as a shock to some saved singles, but our primary life purpose is not to get married, have sex, birth kids, purchase a house with a white picket fence and live a life that we consider, happily ever after. For the Spirit filled, born again Christian single, our life's purpose is to become the best that God calla us to be. This will always mean pressing pass the limits of comfort to the risk of uncertainty and trust in God to get us to that next stage in Him.

Before, I purchased my current car; I leased a brand new Cadillac CTS (a gift that I leased for myself for graduating with my Bachelor's Degree). At the end of my lease, I told God that I was satisfied. I had purchased my "dream car" and now I was just going to get a fifteen hundred dollar get-me-there, so that I could focus my finances toward Jai's high school graduation. This seemed like the wise thing to do. As I was looking for my hooptie (slang for a used vehicle) and prepared to turn my lease in, the Lord began to challenge my logic for settling for my clunker of a car.

"Why do you want to get a fifteen hundred dollar get-me-there?" God asked.

"So that I can get ready for Jai's graduation, get out of debt, and save some money," I responded.

"No, you don't want to use wisdom as it pertains to your money. You are trying to put yourself in a position where you don't have to trust me." God said quite candidly.

I had no words behind God's response. It was true. While on the surface it appeared that my motives for getting a rundown vehicle was to use sound money practices, the truth was I had grown weary in trusting God and wanted to take a hiatus in my faith. As a bird strategically prepares her nest for the comfort of her new brood, I was preparing my life for what I considered the ease of a life devoid of the trust in God, needed to passionately pursue purpose.

We Can't Use Wisdom Without Taking Risks

L ike I began to do, a lot of saved singles walk around like second hand citizens because of their marital state. They hide behind the excuse of wisdom and making sound decisions to stay attached to people, places, and things that God has long called them away from. They let their spiritual, relational, financial, and physical appearance fall by the waste side. All in all, they become content with mediocrity. They lose their luster for life.

While we should use wisdom and solid decision making practices to guide our lives, we cannot afford to mask our lives purpose behind these principles and sacrifice becoming all that God has called us to be. As faith without works is dead (James 2:26), using wisdom without a willingness to take Godly risks, leads us to an empty and unproductive life. Instead of our single state making us the breeding ground as the most productive, successful individuals on earth, we succumb to just being average. Sexual temptation diminishes in our pursuit of purpose as we are so about our life's destiny that sexual temptation has no entrance into our lives.

Revisit Purpose And Never Let Go!

D o any of the examples I've used describe you? Are you unhappy with your current position in life? Have you replaced a passionate pursuit of purpose for status quo? Is your life's focus to get married? Or are you one who has grown tired of believing God for your mate because up until now he or she has not manifested in your life? If your answer is yes to any of these questions it's time for you to revisit purpose; and never let it go!

What dream has God placed in your heart but you've allowed it to die because you don't want to utilize your faith to bring it to pass? What is it that you've always wanted to be when you grew up but have convinced yourself that it's not for you? Maybe you feel that you didn't come from the right ethnicity or you may think that you were born on the wrong side of the tracks? Has your dream always been to become a doctor but you have defaulted to a life of misery by working a factory job that you hate because it's seems to be the road with the least risk? Do you have a desire to be a business owner but lack the knowledge and funds to get started?

Your answers to these inquiries are designed to get you back on the road to a passionate pursuit of purpose. I often say that life is a balancing act where we have to consistently and simultaneously work reality while building our dreams, until our dreams become our reality. Usually singles find themselves on one extreme of the reality-dream spectrum. They are either working reality, by entering the rat race of life. They work to pay bills while barely getting by. This forces their dreams to lay dormant on the side lines of life where they never come to fruition. Some of single saints spend so much time building their dreams that they neglect reality, until life caves in on them and they are forced to face truth. Equilibrium comes into play and a passionate pursuit of purpose surfaces when singles keep both their dreams and reality as the center of their attention. Dreams and reality should both be given an equal amount of our attention until dreams and reality collide, and purpose is birthed.

You see there is nothing wrong with working a job, or living in a home that you don't particularly like for a season, while in the passionate pursuit to purpose. I will talk more about dating in the next Secret of Celibacy entitled "Have Fun But Don't Give 'em None: Dating God's way." For now, I just want to say that there is nothing wrong with dating multiple prospects in the pursuit to Mr. or Mrs. Right (as long as you're honest). All of these situations and relationships are designed to prepare you for purpose in the form of your dream job, dream home, and/or dream mate. Knowing this fact, keeps us focused and avoids us from becoming shipwrecked in spirit when things don't work out as planned.

A passionate pursuit of purpose is more of a mindset in our journey to becoming all that God has called us to be than it is a place of destination. Having the right train of thought on our road to the passionate pursuit of purpose keeps us fueled for the trip. Once we have arrived to one place in purpose, this positive way of thinking prepares us for and propels us into our next voyage on the path in purpose. As a result, we never become stagnate, side tracked, or discontent during our ride.

SECRET

#5

Have Fun, But Don't Give 'Em None: Dating God's Way

Traditional Daters

For simplicities sake I have put dating into two categories:

1. Traditional Daters
2. Liberal Daters

Traditional daters will generally date one person at a time. Their goal is to see if the relationship is what they want. Once their goal is discovered, they move forward either to marriage or to end the relationship. Traditionalists usually date for long periods of time at least a year or two before they decide if the person that they are seeing will be, "the one." Even though their waiting time is lengthy their objective is normally, date to marry. This is how our parents and/or grandparents typically dated. The disadvantage, if any, to the traditional dater is they risk the chance of missing out on other options in choosing a mate because they date fewer people. The good thing about this dater is that they are focused and know what they want, marriage from the relationship.

Liberal Daters

L iberalists on the other hand are comfortable with dating two or three people at one time for short or long intervals. They are not as concerned about being married. Their goal is simply to enjoy the thrill of meeting and going out with different people. They are very social and are what I call the new way of dating. This type of dating has just surfaced within the last decade with the rise of Internet dating. The downside (if any) of a liberal dater would be that their affection seems to be all over the place because they hold multiple interests. Being a liberal dater should not be confused with having multiple sex partners, or playing games. This type of dater simply openly "befriends" more than one person at a time.

The traditionalist are extremely committed and loyal individuals that may look at liberals as being loose and too free spirited when it comes to dating. Not in a bad way, but they are not comfortable with the way that liberals do things and likewise liberals are not comfortable with how traditionalist court. Liberalist may look at conventionalist as being starchy, too serious, and afraid to try new and different things. I would like to mention that there is no right or wrong dating style. As long as both individuals are upfront about their intentions for the relationship, either dating style is acceptable. No matter if you hold to a conventional way of dating or are laissez-faire in your dating style there are some guidelines that should be adhered to in Christian dating.

Believers should have fun and date but we cannot adopt the world's view of dating by dishonoring God, ourselves, and those who are watching us. We have to know:

- Why we are dating.
- How to weather the four seasons of dating.
- Who to date.
- When to date
- Where to date
- What it means to place proper boundaries when dating.
- How to recover when we have become discouraged and decided to ditch dating.

Why Should Christians Date?

The two major reasons why Christians should date are:

> 1. To form friendships.
> 2. To determine if the potential date has what it takes to become their mate.

The dating process although exciting and stimulating should be one of character investigation. When Christians date we should be focusing on getting to know our prospects spiritually and relationally (relevantmagazine.com, retrieved 10/2/13). We should **never** date to fulfill our sexual desires. Regardless if we decide to friend or make the person our life partner in holy matrimony, our ultimate goal in dating should be to build up and make the other person better, while being enhanced ourselves. This is where the concept of "Having fun but don't give 'em none" comes from.

No matter if my daughter, a friend, or me myself are contemplating a dating relationship, one of the first things that I remind them and myself is to, "Have fun but don't give 'em none." It is my way of keeping everyone involved grounded and focused on our reason for dating: to enjoy the experience while checking to see if the other person fits the bill according to God's Word. When this happens, we are able to be objective and build the other person up while growing at the same time.

This win-win dating concept of increasing the value of our date while growing involves both parties making one another feel as if they are entirely what God calls them to be, without the pressure of being involved sexually. While in our dateless phase, we find out what we like as individuals. When we come into the dating phase of our lives, it is our opportunity to find out who the other person is. We discover what they enjoy. Finally, we decide if we are willing to be the one that God uses to fulfill their joy. We determine if we will be the person that cultivates them to be their best selves in marriage.

There is nothing that I like more than being in a romantic relationship. I love being on the arm of a handsome man of God where I feel safe, secure, and free to be me. I enjoy having doors opened for me, chairs pulled out for me, receiving flowers/gifts, and all of the other things that come along with dating. I equally enjoy making a man feel like a man. I like displaying appreciation, by cooking and cleaning (if the relationship has advanced to this point), praying with and for him, and joking with him. In addition, I love giving sincere compliments, making decisions with him, or giving something as small a warm smile to brighten his day. What I like most about dating is the friendship and companionship that comes along with being connected to someone of the opposite sex.

When we have one or two people who are not equally concerned about making each other needs a priority, the relationship is destined to fail. Because we are single Christians, these needs should have nothing to do with having sex. The only sexual need that we should be meeting during the dating relationship is the need to keep one another, "sexually safe" (a term that I use to mean sexually pure).

Meeting the other person's needs could be something as little as needing a couple of hours or a day away from one another to meet a project deadline (or assisting in meeting the deadline). It could also mean a random good morning phone call to bless one another's day with prayer. It could also mean being sensitive enough to ask where the other person would like to eat, if we are always the one who chooses the restaurant. Two Christian adults in a relationship should be able to discuss their needs with one another without feelings of hurt, rejection, and or manipulation.

When you have two people with the same goal to build each other up, God is pleased. You become an example to the world of genuine Christian dating; and you are building your relationship on the rock of God's Word. This gives the relationship the ability to withstand the four seasons of dating and/or storms of life should you decide to marry, *Matthew 7:24-27*. The four seasons of dating are called Ecstasy, Reality, Challenge, and Resolution (Stages of Relationships, 2001).

Ecstasy

During the ecstasy stage those involved in the dating relationship are in sheer bliss. Ecstasy could last as little as one week and as long as a year. This is where you wonder, "Where have you been all of my life?" You feel as if the person you are dating has no flaws and are convinced that this is the one that you will marry. This is my least favorite stage in dating. I am a person who likes to have a grip on my emotions. It is during this stage in the dating process that I feel as if I am somewhat out of control. At times I feel as if I am on an upward roller coaster that refuses to come down.

While I have learned to enjoy this stage, some of the steps that I take to keep me grounded are:

- Constant prayer to God about what's really going on in the relationship.
- An ongoing pursuit of my God given purpose outside of the dating relationship.
- Continuing to keep and cultivate friendships outside of my date.
- Remaining accountable to someone I trust.

Adhering to these safeguards helps to keep me on the track to celibacy and lessens the pain in the event that the relationship does not work out.

When we begin to date, so many times as single Christians we stop living, pursuing God, and personal interests. When the relationship does not work out, we are left lonely and devastated because we've poured all of ourselves in a relationship that did not work. Along with finding help to heal our broken hearts, we have to rediscover God, purpose, and our friends that we put on the back burner to pursue a dating relationship. A new relationship is fun and adventurous but should be tempered with reality as we progress.

Reality

The reality stage is the process in dating where the newness of the relationship is beginning to wear off. We begin to see the imperfections of our date (and they in us). While we are still excited about the relationship, for the first time, we wonder is this person really as good as he or she first seemed. The answer is probably, "No." They have always been the person that we are beginning to see. We either chose to ignore the imperfections, they were hiding them, or the opportunity had not permitted itself for us to see their flaws. In any case, this is why we are not to play Russian roulette with our hearts. Playing hit or miss during the ecstasy stage, by having sex because we think this is our life partner, will only leave us waking up to reality with a challenge. We are left with the challenge of wondering, "What on earth have I gotten myself into?"

Challenge

During the challenge stage is where the two people in the dating relationship are presented with a test of some type to see if the bond can withstand it. This test could be a financial problem, blended family issues, personality conflict or a combination of the three. This is where those involved take a somber assessment of the truth discovered in the reality stage and asks, "Can I deal with this for the rest of my life?" This is not the time that we should use all of our time and energy trying to change the person to who we want them to be. Nor is it the time, to ignore all the warnings that have surfaced to show who the other person really is. We also cannot adopt the false notion that we are going to find a perfect person and run at the first sign of trouble that emerges in the relationship. It is a time to take an honest appraisal of the truth to determine, if we want to move forward. Knowing the presence of reality or challenges does not make either person involved a bad person. The only purpose of the reality and challenge stage is to investigate the truth about the relationship. This helps the couple to make a resolution as to where the relationship is headed.

Resolution

The resolution stage is the proceeding stage of the relationship. It is where the couple determines, if they will advance the connection to engagement/marriage or end it as friends. There is not a whole lot of explanation that the marriage/engagement decision needs. If we decide that we will remain connected and/or exchange nuptials, we go on and prepare to spend the rest of our lives together. Please note that committing to marry and actually being married are not the same. This is not the time to compromise our decisions to remain sexually pure because we have decided to get married. We must continue to honor God with our choice to remain sexually pure until marriage.

When we decide to marry, is when some single saints get into trouble, by deciding that we need to test drive or get training in the sex bed. We reason that we want to make sure everything is attuned. This is immature, shallow, and a poor excuse to operate in the lust of our flesh. We are by nature sexual beings. As my Pastor often states, "Birds don't need flying lessons to fly, and fish don't need swim lessons to swim." I say, (as sexual beings) "People don't need sex lessons to figure out how sex works." Trust me, when the time is right (in the marriage covenant) we will not need any instructions on how to perform. Love making will come naturally and everything will work out fine. Until we have made our date our mate, we are to honor God, ourselves, and our date in maintaining an oath of purity.

If the resolution comes to the point where one or both parties has decided to end the relationship, because we have not slept with one another it makes it a little easier to move on. Any time we spend an excessive amount of intimate time with someone, even when we don't have sex, we take the risk of becoming attached to the person. Although we have not slept with the person, there will still have to be some time of healing of our minds, wills, and emotions from the break up. We may not be able to talk every day or spend time together like we did in the past, but should walk away with a level of respect for ourselves and the other person for our decision to honor God in your bodies. This is the ultimate level of maturity in a dating relationship.

While dating we get so excited during the ecstasy stage of our relationship that we forfeit the time needed to progress through the other three stages. God did not mean for us to mate everyone that we date. We want to keep the primary purpose for courting, to become friends and determine if the other person is our life partner, in the forefront of our minds. This helps us to remain focused and prevents discouragement if the relationship doesn't end with an exchange of wedding vows.

Personally, I like to look at the relationships that I have been in that did not work out as seed sown. Rather than get discouraged about how many relationships I've been in that turned out not to be "the one." I use the associations, in what seems as failures, as God's way of depositing into me the things needed for the "real one." This allows me to credit these men with the things they'll need to be the husbands that God calls them to be to their future wives. I carry this out by putting up a practical yet high standard, to be the best example of a Godly woman that I can be. I do this by being honest, not sleeping with him, and having a whole lot of fun without giving 'em none.

In the event that the guy that I'm dating decides that I am not what he wants or if I decide that he is not what I want, because:

- I have not succumb to my lower nature and slept with him.
- I have learned to take the experience as a seed sown to God for the next woman that this man will date or marry.
- I have followed the 7-Secrets outlined in this book.
- I have encouraged my date to be his best person.

I am able to boldly remind God of His Word, "Do not be deceived God is not mocked, whatever a man sows that shall he also reap *(Galatians 6:7)*. I can tell God with confidence, "God I sow this relationship to you. Because I have not sown to my flesh but the spirit, I expect to get back multiplied what I have sown. This thought pattern gives me a confidence and excitement to wait on Gods best with patient enthusiasm.

Who Should Christians Date?

Now that we are informed about why we date and have weathered the four seasons of the dating relationships, we are ready to know who we should date. As Christians we should not be caught up with superficial prerequisites for dating as age (as long as they are legal), outer appearances, height, level of intelligence, race, social class, income bracket, etc. While these things are important on an individual basis, they are considered personal preferences and not biblical requirements that we should solely base our decision to date on.

The only God requirement that Christians have in dating is that they date other Believers. When taking into consideration if a person is date worthy, the first thing you want to know is your prospect saved, for real! I know everybody deserves to be ministered to and should not be judged, but as born again believers we should NOT be going around missionary dating (dating unsaved men and women with the goal of getting them saved). We are not to be unequally yoked together with unbelievers *(II Corinthians 6:14)*.

An unbelieving interest has no clue of what it takes to be saved so he or she encourages us to skip church. They don't understand our position on biblical obligations such as paying tithes. They definitely are not in agreement with us living a holy and sex free life. Before long we will water down our relationship with God to the point that we are no longer concerned about the things God is concerned about, and we find ourselves in a backslidden state.

When we date someone who is saved, for real, our views are the same and we are not pressured to compromise our sexual integrity. I want to add that just because a person goes to church, sings in the choir, and can quote a couple of scriptures DOES NOT mean that they are really saved. That is why it is important that we test the spirit before we get our spirits, souls, and bodies involved in a relationship. To sum things up, everyone that we date is not our mate and that is why we should wait (until marriage to have sex).

When Should Christians Date?

Christians are ready to date when we are completely able to be ourselves with ourselves, God and others. We must be whole. So many people jump from relationship to relationship when they have never truly been single. They don't know the types of places they like to hang out at, the foods they like to eat, or clothes they like to wear because all of these decisions have been made based on the opinions of those that they have dated. We should only date others when we have adequately dated ourselves. We should know what it's like to plan a trip on our own, by ourselves flowers, both expensive and inexpensive gifts, and go to a movie, out to eat or a basketball game solo and feel comfortable with it.

148

I am not discounting the fact that two is better than one *(Ecclesiastes 4:9)* but if we are in a single state we may as well maximize and enjoy it. During our time of singleness, we have to know what it is that we like to do before we get involved with another who doesn't know what they like. In this case, both parties is trying to influence each other to like something that neither is sure about.

Dating ourselves help us get accustomed to showering ourselves with nice things before some man or woman comes along and starts showering us with gifts and we potentially lose our mind because we don't know how to act. When we are accustomed to dating ourselves and buying ourselves nice things, our attitude is different towards the situation when someone comes along and starts to give us gifts and affection. While we are appreciative and thankful, we are already accustomed to receiving nice things. We are not easily distracted. We are able to focus. We are not simply focused on the gifts that they bare, but we are able to determine if the person is a person of character.

Where To Date And Setting Proper Boundaries

Where single saints decide to go on a date is solely and completely up to the individuals involved. Depending on our budget, the stage of the relationship, and individual preferences, a date may be as simple as attending a play at a local theater. We may want to stop for coffee at a local coffee house after the theater. A date could also be as extravagant as planning a daytrip to a different region such as Paris, France or Venice, in Italy to have lunch and visit the country's main attractions.

Where we go on a date is not as important as having boundaries set in place. Boundaries ensure that we do not succumb to sexual temptation. Because we have developed discipline and identified our hotspots, we know how to prevent from making provisions for our flesh. When we are dating and are beginning to feel emotionally and sexually stirred by the other person, or the mere idea of dating is the time to talk about our feelings and our sexual triggers **thoroughly** with God.

We have to practice foresight and be honest. This is carried out by telling God what we are feeling, what could happen good or bad if He does not give us a way of escape and find out what His Word says about the situation. We have to let God know that everything in us wants to have sex (if that is how we are feeling), but that we want-to-want-to please Him (want-to-want-to is not a typographical error). Sometimes when our wills are set to do the opposite of God's Word, we have to want-to-want-to before we actually get to the place that God's will is a genuine desire of ours.

Finally, we have to allow God to give us a plan and follow it. Ladies, if our "hot spot" is being wined and dined we may want to postpone dates that put us in this position. If God leads us to talk to our date about the way we are feeling if they are mature in their faith they will understand. They won't feel offended when we ask if it's okay if we go on a date out to breakfast and afterwards go with the church evangelism team in outreach, rather than to a candle lit dinner and a movie to further feed our hot spots.

Brothers, if your "hot spot" is a woman catering to you, by cooking for you, you may want to suggest doing something else other than a candle lit dinner under the moon at her house on the patio. Talk it out with God. It does not make you a punk if you place guards in the relationship. Having boundaries makes you a man (of God). I know that it is said that a man wants a woman who is not easy, but there is something to be said about a man who is strong enough to say no to the lust of his flesh.

Remember the purpose of the whole dating experience is character investigation. When God leads us to talk to man or woman about our "hot spot" and they proceed to do things that tempt us, that person is probably not the person that God has designed for us. We can't continue to place ourselves in harm's way. Our job is to immediately, call the relationship off, get back to passionately pursuing purpose, and allow the other person time to grow. If they grow, God will show their hearts by their actions. They will be truly repentant, and will do whatever it takes to please God and make us comfortable in the relationship again. We cannot attempt to make a lesson a blessing. We must chalk the experience up as a lesson, move on and wait for our blessing to arrive.

When I am dating, I have a very few trusted friends that I can run things by to help me stay on the road to celibacy. If I know that my hot spot is triggered and I am attracted to my date sexually, I notify one or all of these friends to let them know what I am feeling so that I am accountable. If I know that I am going to be alone with him in closed quarters, I especially let them know so that they can pray.

Having safeguards and accountability does not make singles any less of an adult and it is not putting people in our business as some would think. It is simply a preventative measure that keeps us out of sexual sin and from possibly marrying the wrong individual. We don't have to tell those that we are accountable to everything that we do with our date. My accountability crew is saved, mostly married, or have been married and know exactly what it's like to dodge the sexual temptations of dating; they already understand and I don't have to do a lot of explaining. Sometimes all that needs to be said is, "I will be alone with him/her at their house tonight, please pray." This is enough to strengthen our spirit and put your flesh on notice that we are accountable.

How To Recover After You Have Ditched Dating

Now that we know the why, who, when, and where of dating while setting proper boundaries, and how to get through the stages of dating, I would like to address those singles who have given up on courting all together. Whether you are a traditional or liberal dater, this section is designed for those who have been hurt and wounded by the dating scene. This is for singles who have become discouraged in seeking a mate because they have not been able to find "the one." I would like to share with this group how to properly recover after they have become dismayed with dating. I have gleaned some of the practices used by the Prophet Samuel as he was looking for the new king of Israel amongst the sons of Jesse.

Samuel's Standard In Choosing A King

*A*nd Samuel came no more to see Saul until the day of his death: nevertheless Samuel mourned for Saul and the Lord repented that he had made Saul king over Israel.

Now the LORD said to Samuel, "How long will you mourn for Saul, seeing I have rejected him from reigning over Israel? Fill your horn with oil, and go; I am sending you to Jesse the Bethlehemite. For I have provided Myself a king among his sons."
² And Samuel said, "How can I go? If Saul hears it, he will kill me."

But the LORD said, "Take a heifer with you, and say, 'I have come to sacrifice to the LORD.' ³ Then invite Jesse to the sacrifice, and I will show you what you shall do; you shall anoint for Me the one I name to you." ⁴ So Samuel did what the LORD said, and went to Bethlehem. And the elders of the town trembled at his coming, and said, "Do you come peaceably?" ⁵ And he said, "Peaceably; I have *come to sacrifice to the LORD. Sanctify yourselves, and come with me to the sacrifice."*

Then he consecrated Jesse and his sons, and invited them to the sacrifice. [6] So it was, when they came, that he looked at Eliab and said, "Surely the LORD's anointed is before Him!" [7] But the LORD said to Samuel, "Do not look at his appearance or at his physical stature, because I have refused him. For the LORD does not see as man sees; for man looks at the outward appearance, but the LORD looks at the heart."[8] So Jesse called Abinadab, and made him pass before Samuel. And he said, "Neither has the LORD chosen this one." [9] Then Jesse made Shammah pass by. And he said, "Neither has the LORD chosen this one." [10] Thus Jesse made seven of his sons pass before Samuel. And Samuel said to Jesse, "The LORD has not chosen these." [11] And Samuel said to Jesse, "Are all the young men here?" Then he said, "There remains yet the youngest, and there he is, keeping the sheep."

And Samuel said to Jesse, "Send and bring him. For we will not sit down till he comes here." [12] So he sent and brought him in. Now he was ruddy, with bright eyes, and good-looking. And the LORD said, "Arise, anoint him; for this is the one!" [13] Then

Samuel took the horn of oil and anointed him in the midst of his brothers; and the Spirit of the LORD came upon David from that day forward. So Samuel arose and went to Ramah. (I Samuel 15:35; 16:1-13)

Although this story is the account of the Prophet Samuel's response to King Saul being overthrown from his position as ruler over Israel, single believers can draw a lot from the episode. Like some singles that have experienced one break up after the other, Samuel was extremely heartbroken about Israel's loss of Saul as king to the point that he mourned the loss of Saul. Notice, that although Samuel grieved Saul's absence, he resisted the temptation to take matters into his own hands by trying to reconcile Saul to his prior position as king. I Samuel 15:35 states, Samuel did not go to see him again until Saul's death.

After processing through the stages of the relationship and coming to the point that we know it's over, it's time to move on with our lives and away from the relationship. During this time, it is very tempting to keep going back to try and make the relationship work. Don't get me wrong, I am aware that during this time God will sometimes move on the hearts of both individuals to the point that they discover that they were meant to be together. Those are not the cases that I speak of. I think it is normal, for a period in the resolution stage, to break off the relationship for a brief time to allow ourselves to see what it is that we want and to hear from God.

But when we know that we know, that our know-knows, that it's time to move on we have to stop revisiting old, dead relationships with the hope that God will somehow resurrect something that has been long dead.

God Has A Mate For You

Like Samuel some single saints spend months, years, even a life time trying to overcome the sorrow caused by a break up.

If this is you, God is saying to you as he said to Samuel, "How long will you mourn over that relationship that didn't work? I have rejected them as King (your spouse). Regain your joy and go out and date, getting to know others of like precious faith until I reveal to you the one that I have provided as your mate."

If it is your desire to get married, God has a mate for you. You cannot afford to grow weary in well doing *(Galatians 6:9)*. Your challenge is to get over the hurt and take the risk of getting back into the dating game. Like Samuel, some of your responses may be how can I go and date again when I have been hurt? The next person may hurt me, too. God is saying go and date anyway. When you do this you may have to go through a few dates before finding your king or queen but do not be discouraged. Prior to finding the king of Israel, Samuel interviewed seven of Jesse's sons before God revealed Israel's next ruler.

As God did for Jesse to recognize the next king, He is sharpening your spiritual senses to recognize his best for your life.

Initially, Samuel just knew that the first of Jesse's sons, Eliab would be the nation's next emperor. He had the look of a king, he may have walked like the king, having all the right education and training; but God encouraged Samuel, not to look at his outward appearance because He had rejected him. He continued to tell him that man looks at the outward appearance but I (God) looks at the heart.

God wants us looking at the heart of the man or woman that we date as well. We are not to choose our mates primarily on looks, their financial status, or even their position in the church; we are to choose the mate that God has for us based solely upon where their heart is toward God.

Determining A Person's Heart Towards God

We determine a person's heart towards God by taking time to look past our emotions, or what our natural eye can see and look at their character:

- Do they keep their word?
- Are they as saved around family and friends as they are in church?
- How do they respond to ordained authority?

- How do they treat their parents?
- Do they arrive to work and on dates on time?
- When they are going to be late, do they call ahead to make amends?
- Do they pay their tithes and give offerings or are they considered God robbers according to Malachi 3:9-10.
- When the two of you are on a date are they constantly pressuring you for sex or putting you in compromising positions?
- Is what important to you important to them or are they secretly selfish?

The answers that come out of this inward analysis of a date are how we discover who he or she really is. The responses help us to determine if the person that we are in relationship with is saved, for real. This character quiz should not be limited to just our date. This should be a win-win experience. While we are checking out our date you should also be finding out more about ourselves. I have made some awesome discoveries about myself during the dating process, both good and bad.

Pray For A Plan

One time while dating when my daughter was younger I found that she was having a really hard time adjusting to my new relationship. She had been so used to it being just she and I along with the fact that she loved her daddy, that she became quite comfortable with the way things were. When this new guy came along she just did not adjust well. By nature, she is a very mild mannered, even tempered, and beautifully spirited person. When she began to treat my date mean and rude, I was very concerned. When the relationship ended (not because of anything that she did) I used this time to better prepare her and myself for my husband.

I used the time to pray for a plan, build up her self-esteem, talk to her often about the fact that one day someone would come into our lives. I also let her know how she fit into the whole scheme of things. This drew us both closer to God and one another. When I got into relationships later I could see that she was more confident in her role because of this time of preparation, as we did not have all the drama that we had experienced previously.

Prematurely having sex with our date blinds us to all the tell-tale signs of who they really are, and who we are. God's Word says, "If any of you lack wisdom, let him ask" *(James 1:5)*. When we ask God to reveal our date's character to us, He will do it. He will not make the choice for us, however. It is our responsibility to properly process through the dating cycle so that we can make an educated choice.

Get Back Into The Dating Game

While I love couples who have dated and have the traditional testimony that they have only dated each other and had to look no further because they knew that their spouse was the one, the truth is this doesn't happen as often as it did in times past. To get back into the game of dating and move on with our lives, we may have to become more liberal (without sexual compromise) in our dating style before God reveals to us "the one." We cannot allow hurt and disappointments to deter us from seeking out a happy life with another, if that is what we desire.

Outside of the fact that premarital sex forfeits God's best in our lives, the bitter truth is upon entering a relationship we really have no clue as to who the person that we are dating really is (even if we are somewhat familiar with them), if we are genuinely compatible with the other person, or if they will be around long. For these reasons we should always look at the person we are dating as a brother or sister in Christ. A sane person would not have sex with his or her natural sibling and we should not be sexing our spiritual siblings. This is called spiritual incest.

Keeping Sober Minded

Until I say, "I do" anytime that I am in a relationship I always keep in the back of my mind that tomorrow my feelings or his could change, the relationship may be over, and it is possible that I may see him with another sister one day. No, I am not planning the demise of the relationship, I just want to keep myself sober minded during the process and have the ability to hold my head up. I want to have the ability to love on both him and her in the event the relationship does not work. This is a time where I keep my feet planted, eyes opened and legs closed.

Even when sex is not a part of the equation, being at peace with an ex and their new love interest is a challenge. When we have sexed our date, walking in love toward an them and their new love is nearly impossible. Instead of loving on the two when we see them out we are rolling your eyes at them, keying cars, flattening tires, stalking their homes, and social media sites, blowing up their phones, and just acting a jealous mess.

But when we have kept our sexual passions on lock down, God will strengthens us to be able to see him or her with their new Boo, smile and say, "Hi, God bless you. It was really nice to see you." While we may be extremely hurt afterward, and may even shed a few tears (later when no one is watching) we have handled the situation like a real man or woman of God. We go away with a level of self-respect.

Our bodies are our business. Good business men and women never allow their emotions to determine the outcome of a business transaction. Likewise, during the dating process, we should not allow our emotions to cloud our vision of what is really going on in the relationship. This mindset gives us the freedom to have fun in a dating relationship without the pressure of having to give into sexual temptation. It allows us to enjoy the development of forging friendships with the opposite sex, minus the heart break in the event the relationship doesn't work out. Finally, it allows us to truly and freely give The Lord our God "that" part of our heart.

SECRET

#6

Give HIM 'That' Part Of Your Heart

During our state of singleness, it's as if we are (almost unconsciously) waiting on that special someone that we can share our everything with in order to experience true satisfaction in our lives. We have dreams of the perfect lover that we can tell our most intimate secrets, without the fear of betrayal. We imagine a life with a spouse with whom we can be our true selves, absent the apprehension of judgment. We have fantasies of being the perfect pair that all other couples want to mimic or be like.

In and of itself there is nothing wrong with these relational aspirations with the mate of our dreams. The challenge that we encounter is that we sometimes limit our relationship with God with this type of thinking. When as singles, we put our hearts on hold for someone outside of God, we set ourselves up for disappointment. God did not fashion any other human being or object to fulfill us completely. Although it is not our intention, we postpone happiness with the only true source that can bring us joy, for an idealistic connection with another human. The joy of the Lord is our strength *(Nehemiah 8:10)*. When we depend and count on outside sources as our strength, we become disillusioned when the other person is unable to fulfill our false expectations.

One day while moping to God over a failed relationship that I really wanted to work, I complained, "God, how could the relationship turn out like this? I mean, I love him. I gave myself to him (not sexually but of my time and heart)," I continued to rant.

"God, I mean I told him that I loved him, and that I didn't want to be without him and this is how it turns out? I don't understand."

Pouring Myself Into The Relationship

While meditating on all of the ways that I had really poured myself into the relationship like I had been unwilling to do in other romantic relationships, I thought about how I rearranged my busy schedule to be with him when he wanted to see me, or I wanted to see him. I pondered on how I was willing to stay up with him during all times of the night and morning to talk on the phone about everything and nothing. I continued to think about how I allowed his interests to become my interests, even if I did not particularly like his interests. I enjoyed praying with him and for him. I wanted to cook for him, hold his hand, laugh with him, and do all the things that a person does when they are in love.

My heart would skip a beat when he entered the room, as I was happy in his presence, sad to see him leave, and willing to do just about anything to make him smile. During this time of deep reflection, God interrupted my thoughts and told me,
"I want 'that' part of your heart."

A sense of sadness and relief came over me. I was sad because without knowing it, for the first time I had gotten side tracked in giving a man a part of me that was fashioned specifically for God. The sadness that I experienced was not a condemnation/guilt type sorrow. It was the sort of sorrow that said,

"I'm sorry that I unknowingly hurt you and I want to do whatever it takes to get it right." I was relieved because I realized that God had allowed the beginning and ending of the relationship to take me to a deeper place in Him. I discovered that had it not been for the occurrence of this particular relationship I would not be able to relate to giving God 'that' part of my heart and would not ever truly be ready for a marriage relationship.

Purpose For The Relationship

I now knew the whole purpose for the relationship and was able to more readily accept the process that it would take to overcome the hurt. I knew that God would, over time heal my broken heart and allow love to enter in again, once I understood and became intentional in properly giving Him 'that' part of my heart. Not long after this discovery, I was able to draw some conclusions about what the whole notion of giving Him 'that' part of my heart meant.

We know God has 'that' part of our heart when His interests are our interests, even when we don't particularly like His interest. We want to see Him smile, please Him, be with Him and do whatever it takes to bring joy to His heart. We want to talk to him (in prayer) during all times of the day and night about everything and nothing. Our heart skips a beat in His presence and what makes Him sad, saddens us. While we cannot see God with our natural eye, we experience His presence through the manifestation of His goodness through answered prayer in our lives and the lives of others.

Another lesson that I was able to pull away from this love interest is giving God 'that' part of my heart was not about following some set of strict rules in order to be in relationship with Him. At times we think, because we pray at a certain time in a specific position, using just the right dialogue that we are in relationship with God. We're convinced that we're doing what it takes to please Him. I learned from this relationship that loving God should be spontaneous and fun. That means if I talk (pray) to Him for two minutes or two hours it ought to be meaningful and heartfelt. Whether on my knees at my bedside, lying down, or washing dishes at the kitchen sink, my prayer should be genuine and true.

Matthew 6:33 reminds us that if we first seek God's Kingdom and righteousness that all these things will be added to us (this includes a mate). Nothing pleases God more than seeing a lost soul converted to Christ. We give Him 'that' part of our heart when our mindsets are to win as many souls into the Kingdom of God as we possibly can, not as much by what we say, but by the lives that we lead.

If we are in sexual sin or have an imbalance in our relationships, it shows we have not given God 'that' part of our hearts. In these instances, our lifestyle detracts instead of attracts the lost to Christ. We are not concerned about what God is concerned about. We are only interested in fulfilling the lust of the flesh. The other ways that God gauges if He has 'that' part of our hearts is how we spend our money, time, and display our trust in Him.

Giving

Where your money is there your heart will be also *(Luke 12:34)*. We talked about the importance of the tithe and offering in "Developing Discipline" so I won't go into detail about the subject. I just want to draw the point that to effectively give God 'that' part of my heart, I have to be sure I am paying my tithes and offerings. Remember this book is for believers and or aspiring Christians. I hear so many excuses from Christians as to why they can't be obedient in their giving from fear that the preacher is stealing the money, to the feeling that they cannot afford to pay their tithes and give offerings due to financial hard times. Some Christians will pay their tithes and offerings as long as things "look" good for them financially. As soon as they hit a hard place financially they remove the tithe from their budget and excuse themselves stating things like, "God understands."

This shows immaturity and a lack of true trust in God. We are to walk by Faith and not by sight in financial tough times, *(II Corinthians 5:7)*. Tithing is a God idea and not a man idea. When we become born again Christians, we exchange our way of doing things for God's way. If you are in a church where you can't trust the man and/or woman of God with your giving, you need to do one of two things:

- Earnestly pray and ask God to help you to overcome the fear and lie that all men and/or women of God can't be trusted.
- If you **know** that the leadership in your church is stealing money, go to a church where financial integrity is a priority.

Whatever you do, do not use this as an excuse or crutch and miss out on the opportunity to give God 'that' part of your heart in giving you tithe and offerings.

Time

We know God has our heart when we make it a priority to carve out space in our day to spend quality time with Him. Because God is a God of relationship and not religion or strict man made rules, this time should be both planned and spontaneous. We can spend time with God in so many ways like:

- Praying to him
- Praise and worship
- During surprise moments in our day choosing to read scripture during breaks at work, talking to him while doing chores, or during our commute to and from work.

Just as we don't allow life to prevent us from spending time with our natural love interests, we cannot allow distractions to keep us from spending adequate time with God.

Trust

Getting our heart condition to line up with God's Word is one of the final steps that God uses to know when He can bless us with His best in the area of a mate. Until God has 'that' part of our heart he cannot trust us with a mate. He knows we are at risk of making our spouses our God. Giving Him 'that' part of our heart helps God know that we are mature enough to handle a relationship. Winning souls into the kingdom and how we spend our time and money is the measuring stick that God uses to determine if we have the proper perspective of what He considers a healthy marriage relationship. He knows that when we have given Him 'that' part of our heart, as the time comes for us to get married, we will not look to our spouses with unrealistic expectations. We will not depend on our mates to fill voids in our lives that only God can fill. Giving God 'that' part of our heart shows that we can be

170

trusted with the emotions of another because God is truly on the throne of our heart.

If we want God's best in the area of a mate, God has to have 'that' part of our heart. God has no problem with us giving our love to the objects of our affection, here on earth. Our main priority must be God's main priority, first.

While I was in this particular relationship that I mentioned at the beginning of this chapter, I realized that although I had been kingdom conscious about winning souls to the kingdom, I spent time with God, gave of my tithe and offerings to my local church, and made time for God throughout my day to day life, I became out of balance in these areas. Although I was going through the motions and my main priority was to please God, I realized I had some growing to do because it was more difficult to keep this perspective. God is a jealous God *(Deuteronomy 6:15)*. He will not allow anyone to share 'that' part of our hearts that was fashioned specifically for Him.

I discovered through this dating experience what also pleases God is when we have reached the point that we show total trust in our pursuit of Him.

The entire premise for "The 7-Secrets of Celibacy: The Single Christians Guide on How to Wait on A Mate" is about building a relationship with God and constructing all other unions that we are involved in around our foundational relationship with God. It is not until we have given God 'that' part of our hearts that we are ready to enjoy a lasting relationship with another human being.

SECRET

#7

Don't Quit

How to Remain Sexually Pure

I'm frequently asked by Singles who are struggling with sexual sin, "How do you do it (remain abstinent)?" Usually I give them an answer full of love and grace encouraging them with responses like, "Don't be so hard on yourself and don't quit! He who began a good work in you shall complete it until the day of Jesus Christ (*Philippians 1:6*). You are a winner!" Singles who struggle with sexual sin sometimes do so because although we know that sex before marriage is wrong, what we don't know is "how" to remain sexually pure.

The third time that Jesus appeared to the disciples after He had risen from the dead, He told Peter three times, "If you love me feed my sheep." It is tempting to interpret this passage as we always do, by looking at the obvious. At first glance it is apparent that Peter is disheartened by Jesus' repetitive questioning of Peter's love for Him *(John 21:17)*. As I began to meditate on this particular passage, I couldn't help but wonder if Peter's discouragement was possibly brought on by the fact that he did not know "how" to feed Jesus' sheep.

Yes, he had walked with Jesus and watched Jesus feed the multitudes with five loaves and two fish *(Mark 6:41)*. He witnessed Jesus pay taxes from money provided out of the mouth of a fish *(Matthew 17:24-27)*. He had even observed Jesus raise a girl from the dead *(Mark 5:37-43)*. Although, we are more prone to gravitate towards the obvious doctrine that Peter was saddened that Jesus

174

would question his love for Him, I believe some of Peter's disappointment may have been rooted in the thought that "Yes, Lord I have seen you feed your sheep and perform countless miracles, but You are supposed to do those things, for You are God. I am mere mortal man. How am I supposed to do what you did?"

Pretty Big Shoes To Fill

P eter had some pretty big shoes to fill and rather than look at who Jesus was on the inside of him, Peter could have been paying more attention to the weakness of his own flesh. It saddened, maybe even overwhelmed him with the thought of having to carry out such a great commission and walk in the footsteps of his sovereign Lord and Savior Jesus Christ, by feeding His sheep.

Singles are no different. When God tells singles, "If you love me, obey me (John 14:15) and stop sinning sexually." Because sex is such a beautiful experience that most enjoy, we become discouraged thinking,

"How will I ever be able to resist sexual temptation in my mortal flesh, on my own?"
We reason, "God, I know that You are able to do such a thing, because You are God."

We forget that the greater one lives on the inside of us (I John 4:4). We fail to realize that He who began a good work in us shall complete it until the day of Jesus *(Philippians 1:6)*. We forget to ask God for His wisdom and plan *(James 1:5, Jeremiah 29:11)*.

Once we receive God's wisdom and plan we forget to remain steadfast and not quit.

A Plan

Early on in my road to victory over sexual sin, I adopted the attitude that if God asked me to do something in His Word, then He has to provide me with a plan to help with the task. We ruin our chances at triumph over promiscuity because we quit seeking God for a line upon line, precept upon precept plan for deliverance. One of the major reasons we don't ask God for a plan (outside the fact that we really don't want to come out of sexual sin) is because of subtle pride. Pride goes before destruction and a haughty spirit before a fall *(Proverbs 16:18)*. Prayerlessness is pride. We allow pride to set in when we think like Peter may have thought. He had been walking with Jesus for a while and had seen Him perform countless miracles in his life, and the lives of others. We think we should somehow already know how to quit sinning sexually, when in fact we don't know the first thing about it. Because we don't know how to go about abstaining from sexual sin, we don't humble ourselves and ask God the infamous question, "How?"

Jesus gave singles an example of how to get wisdom in any situation that we may go through during His time on the earth through the discipline of prayer. The Bible is filled with instances where Jesus drew away from the crowd and prayed or where He

176

prayed openly in front of the crowd. Jesus lived a sin free life and was tempted yet without sin because He never quit asking God "How" through prayer.

Become Like Children

We have to become like little children *(Matthew 18:3)* when it comes to our sexual freedom. If you have been around any child around the ages of two to four years old you may have noticed that they want to know the "Why" behind everything. If you tell them not to do something they want to know, "Why?" If you give them your name during a playful conversation they ask, "Why?" When you inform them that it is bed time they ask the legendary question, "Why?" Even though their repetitious "Why" may seem annoying to us and at times we may try to circumvent the conversation, God never tires or tries to evade us during our "Why?" or in this case "How?" moments.

The answer that He gives us may not be what we want to hear, but if we are persistent He will give us a peace about what we don't like or want to hear. We will need resilience in acting on each of the Secrets of Celibacy in order to be successful. We must be patient with ourselves, others, and God in order to be processed out of sexual sin. There is no quick fix to attaining sexual freedom, a tenacious, don't quit attitude is essential to overcoming.

During a conversation with a very special family member of mine, he asked me the question, "How do you get closer to God?"

177

He continued to state, "I'm reading my Bible and praying and doing all that I know to do, but how do I get closer to Him?" Hearing both the sincerity and desperation in his voice to develop a deeper relationship with God, I simply responded, "Don't quit." I continued to tell him, "Keep reading your Word, and praying. Cry out to God about your weaknesses. Stay in God's face."

Staying In God's Face

When overcoming sexual sin, I would like to offer to you, my reader the same advice that I gave to my family member, don't quit! Stay in God's face. Keep practicing the 7-Secrets of Celibacy until they have become engrafted in your heart. God is not a man that He should lie, nor the son of Man that he should repent. He is no respecter of persons *(Acts 10:34)*. You have got to take God at His Word. He said that he will deliver you *(Psalms 71:20)*. Do not tire of asking God how to quit sexual sin, what specific steps will it take for you to quit, and where you can find your deliverance in His Word. Ask Him to give you a revelation, understanding at your level of comprehension of His plan to sexual freedom for your life. Those who come to God must believe that He is and that He rewards those who diligently seek Him *(Hebrews 11:6)*.

So many single believers fall back into sexual sin because they quit on God. They do one of two things. They either become weary of their weakness toward sex, throwing in the towel on themselves and following a sex free lifestyle, or they think that God gets tired of them and gives up on them. Whatever the train of thought, the outcome usually ends up with them retreating back into a defeated lifestyle of fornication.

During my mission toward sexual freedom, I had to practice not quitting. I knew that I needed God. I knew that I could not live without Him. I knew that my sexual sin placed a huge wedge between God and myself. I was desperate to live sexually free. In fact, there was one period in my life where I rededicated my life to Christ seemingly every day because of sexual immorality. Every Sunday, I was back at the altar whenever my pastor had an altar call because I was that serious about becoming sexually free and I realized I could not do it without God.

At home, I would cry out to God and remind Him of His Word to deliver me *(Psalms 71:20)*. People looked at me funny, I felt uncomfortable at first, but I was desperate to be free. I reminded God that I could not free myself and if He wanted me to do His Word (to flee sexual immorality) then, He would have to help me by giving me a plan and showing me how. I told him that His Word said that when I am weak He is strong *(II Corinthians 12:9)*.

I was so tenacious in my chase toward sexual freedom, that I believe that God, Jesus, and The Holy Spirit, gathered the host of angels to conduct a meeting and announced, "Let's deliver this girl so she can leave us alone," because they were tired of me. Of course this is a joke. There is no such thing as God getting tired of us. The point that I am trying to make is in order to walk in your freedom from any form of sin, you will also have to cultivate this type of desperation.

Each person is different, you may not go to the altar each week, but you have to develop a get in your face attitude with God until He delivers you. If you have made it to this section in this book, I want to congratulate you by saying, "Well done!" This is evidence that you do not have any quit in you. Continue to run after God for your deliverance from sexual sin. This will free you up to be all that he has called you to be and prepare you properly to wait on your mate. God bless you!

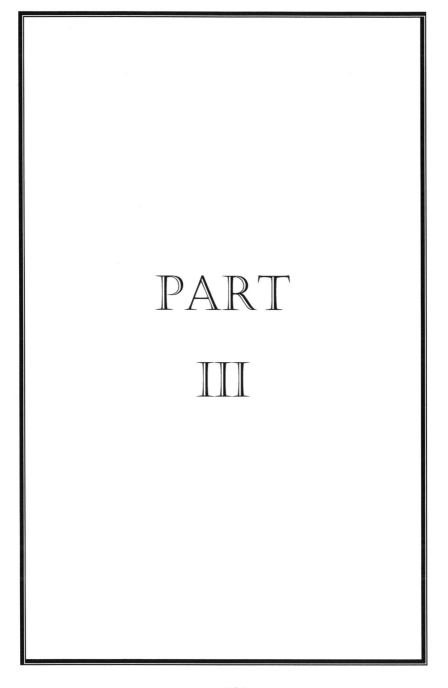

PART

III

1

How to Wait

on a Mate

Born Waiting

While some find waiting for anything an uncomfortable pause in time, I have come to realize that I was born waiting.

In an attempt to play with the rest of her siblings, at age 15, my seven-month pregnant mother, against all conventional wisdom, went rolling down the hill at our local Hoyt Park. Three days later she would find out that her belly-to-back cartwheels had launched her into premature labor. After being rushed to the hospital by her parents, she gave birth to a three pound nine ounce baby girl. Even though I survived my mother's acrobatic stunt, in order to fully develop, I would have to spend the next 45 days of my life in an incubator in the intensive care unit of the hospital.

It goes without saying that I remember nothing about my stay in the hospital except what my mother has told me over the years. I can't help but to believe that those months of waiting served as the foundation for developing patience in me for every other area of my life, including waiting on a mate.

An incubator is used to keep a premature baby in a stable environment while their organs continue to grow outside of the mother's womb. It ensures that sufficient oxygen is getting to the brain, and it helps to protect the baby from obtaining infections that could be fatal to the infant's life.

Welcome The Wait

While some would be tempted to feel sorry for a baby having to be left alone for nearly two months away from her parents, I have come to realize that it was this time that allowed me learn to welcome life's waits. I have had times of pause in my life that would devastate some around me. I have had to wait for justice after being passed over for job promotions. I had to wait 15 years to get my Master's Degree. As the physical head of my household, I had to go to school some semester's full time, while working a full time job, and fulfill responsibilities for other areas of me and my daughter's life. I have been on the brink of marriage a couple times only to be told by God, "No," or "Wait." Even the length of time that it took for me to write this book, I have found myself waiting. While others seemed impatient with me about the time they thought each promise was to be fulfilled in my life and though initially, I have been disappointed, I have always been able to somehow be at ease, relaxed, and comfortable in the wait. It's as if my brain has been hard wired to wait.

Years ago, while trying to rush through a romantic relationship (that I knew was not God), my Mother bluntly reminded me, "You were supposed to be born in November. Every so often around September you get out of God's timing." I don't know if the specific timing of this relationship was in September, but what my Mom was saying is, "Remember you were born prematurely. You have to be conscious to wait. Jumping ahead of

184

God in this relationship may be like an unwise back-to-belly roll down the Hoyt Park hill. Don't jump out ahead of God. You need to spend some time in the incubator waiting. You want to ensure this relationship develops." Instead of getting offended by my mother's synopsis of my situation, I realized that I am most comfortable in the wait.

Once during a different romantic relationship, my Pastor encouraged the young man that I was dating, "If you rush her or move to fast she'll run." My pastor was right. I have come to understand that I am hard wired to wait. No matter the situation, if I feel that I am being rushed out of that incubator before I have had time to develop, (rather in a relationship, business, or personal decision); I am running for my life. Waiting has become a survival tactic for me. Needless to say the guy didn't listen and yes, I ran. Not to try and prove a point that my Pastor was right, but I have just learned from birth that there is wisdom in waiting. I learned as a premature baby that if I am going to survive, I will have to learn to wait.

Developed Character

That time in the hospital as a premature baby not only developed my organs but it developed the character needed to sustain me through life's times of waiting. I have learned not to get jealous while others around me are getting married, being promoted, or launching their careers. Instead they give me hope in

185

which to focus my faith. While all the other babies were being released from the hospital and I had to remain, I can't help but imagine that my little mind and heart fellowshipped with God thinking, "I am next!" If God developed them to where they needed to be while they were in the same state that I am in, then He has to do the same for me! All I have to do is, wait.

If you are going to survive and live a victorious life of celibacy you will also have to work on waiting. Maybe you were not born prematurely and feel like you are just not hard wired to wait. You want what you want and you want it now. There are some situations in your everyday life that you can use to help develop your wait muscle.

When you are in long lines at the grocery store and are tempted to get out of the line into another that "looks" shorter, don't do it. Wait. Nine times out of ten you will find that the people who were behind you in the first line that you jumped out of have been waited on and are on their way out of the store while you are still doing what you did not want to do in the first place: Wait. When you are headed to a friend's house and get caught by a train in route and want to do a U-turn and go the other way, if it is not a 911 emergency, resist the lure to rush and wait. The next time you are on the highway and a car is going what seems to be too slow; instead of going around them, sit back, relax and yes, wait. These situations may seem trivial and insignificant when it comes to waiting on a mate, but if you will commit to putting them to practice, you will find them helpful during your most critical times of delay.

Prison Sentence Or Time Of Preparation?

I realize that not everyone is encouraged by my nearly two decade tenure of no sex. They view the time as a prison sentence rather than look at it as, a blessed time of preparation from The Lord. People ask me all the time,

"So, you ain't married yet?"

They say this as if to say,

"What do I have to be encouraged about? You've been waiting all this time and still haven't received the promise or a husband yet. Why should I be optimistic?"

What they fail to realize is that I understand that a mate is not the promise or prize, I am. Who I am or become, I will attract. I know that the longer that I have waited in God's incubator of singleness, the better I will become and the stronger that my marriage will be. My husband and I will be an extraordinary example to the Body of Christ of what it means to wait on God's best and that alone is enough for me. So what do I say to the doubter, unbeliever, and the skeptic?

"Be not deceived God is not mocked whatsoever a man or woman sows that shall he (she) also reap *(Galatians 6:7)*. Because I have spent nearly 20 years delighting myself in Him in living upright I have a unmovable and unshakeable knowing that God is

187

obligated to give me the desires of my heart in the area of a mate *(Psalms 37:4)*.

Are there times where the devil tries to tell me that God has forgotten about me? Yes, but I don't dwell on his lies. When I am tempted to doubt if God will bless me with a mate, I immediately bring that thought into captivity *(II Corinthians 10:5)* by speaking God's Word over my life and go about fulfilling purpose, having fun, and being the best example of a single Christian that I can be.

According To Your Faith

lease do not let the devil use other well-meaning people, and the length of time you've been waiting to get you off of your square in believing that God has someone fashioned just for you. In His timing, he will draw the two of you together. None will be missing not one will lack her mate for His mouth gave the order and His spirit will draw you together *(Isaiah 34:16)*. Know that the manifestation of God's best for you in the area of a mate is fulfilled according to your faith *(Matthew 9:29)*. If you are wishy-washy by looking at how long you've been waiting for a mate, or go by the negativity of what people say, you cannot properly stand on God's Word for a mate or anything else. The Bible calls people who ask God for something and do not believe that they will receive it, double-minded and unstable. This sort of person cannot expect to receive anything from God *(James 1:5-8)*.

Refocus

Getting back to the original question, how do you wait on a mate? After following the 7-Secrets of Celibacy, the answer is simple; you don't wait on a mate. You wait on the Lord. In Isaiah 40:31 we are reminded, "They that wait upon the Lord shall renew their strength; they shall mount up with wings as eagles; they shall run, and not be weary; and they shall walk, and not faint." The reason that we grow tired and discontent during the process of waiting on a mate is because we have been waiting on the wrong thing, or should I say the wrong person.

Single believers have to get their eyes off of waiting on a mate and refocus to waiting on the Lord. But how do we wait on the Lord, you may ask? This answer is not complicated either. You wait on the Lord by doing those things that please Him. While there are a host of things we can do to please Him as discussed in Secret #6, "Give Him 'That' Part of Your Heart," the primary way that we wait on the Lord is by "Developing in the Disciplines" as outlined in Secret #2 in order to be all that He has called us to be.

Once you have discovered who God is and who you are, your wait on a mate shifts to waiting on the Lord. As you wait on the Lord, you are so busy doing what pleases Him that without knowing it your wait for a mate begins to rest in quiet confidence, great expectation, and joy! You know that He who has promised is faithful *(Hebrews 10:23)*. You are not afraid of sudden terror

189

(Proverbs 3:25) or not ever getting married because you know that you have properly waited on the Lord and in doing so you have prepared your spirit, soul, and body for God's best in the area of a mate.

2

Leaving a Legacy of Celibacy:
A Charge to Parents & Virgins

Parents

Recently my daughter had the opportunity to study at the prestigious Brown University in Providence, Rhode Island for a semester as a visiting student. Before she knew that she would be chosen to attend the fellowship, she was so excited that she began to do some research on Brown's history while finishing the semester at her home college. While picking her up from the train station for a holiday break, she began to tell me some of her new discoveries about the University. During our conversation, she told me, "Ma, I was looking at the roster for the tennis team and it showed that generations of families attend Brown. There are students whose parents and their parents all have graduated from Brown. That is what I want to do. I want to leave a legacy!"

I was so in awe of not only Jai's initiative to investigate the prospective college but I was more impressed with the force that drove her. It was at this moment, without an official yes from the powers that be that I knew in my heart that she would be attending the University the next semester. As a mother, I was so in awe of her response. I knew her motive for wanting to go was not just about going to an Ivy League College for bragging rights or to have something to look good on her resume. I knew that God was going to allow her the experience because she wanted to fulfill purpose. She wanted to leave a legacy that would benefit her children and their children.

The Blessing And The Curse

As I have mentioned before, besides wanting to please God and be an example to my ex-boyfriend, one of the most important reasons that I wanted to maintain a life of celibacy was that I knew that everything that I did Jai was prone to repeat. "I call heaven and earth as witnesses against you this day that I have set before you life and death, the blessing and the curse: therefore *choose life that you and your seed may live*" *(Deuteronomy 30:19)*. I knew that if I could live a celibate life so could my daughter, her children and their children (if they choose to). I could leave a legacy of celibacy.

If you look throughout history, anytime God wanted to usher in a change or blessing to His people, He did it through one person. He used Noah to build an ark to save mankind from God's judgment *(Genesis 5:32-10:1)*. Queen Esther was used to save her people, the Jews from an ethnic genocide *(Esther 81:17)*. A more modern example is the Reverend Martin Luther King Jr. risking his life to deliver racial and civil equality for mankind. God wants to use you and I to stop the transmission of sexual sin throughout the lineage of our families.

Because Satan is a poor counterfeit of God's blessing, he attempts to duplicate God by using one person to continue a curse from generation to generation. The ways that he does this is through our ignorance about our past, and creating a bridge of division between parent and child. People are destroyed for a lack of knowledge *(Hosea 4:6)*. We cannot be ignorant of the enemy's devices or tactics *(II Corinthians 2:11)*. We must first be aware that Satan is trying to continue the curse through our children and their children. Then we must bridge the gap of division between parents and children through what I call relational parenting.

Nothing New Under The Sun

We have got to stop thinking it strange as parents when the enemy uses the familiar spirits of our past to attack our children. Instead, we should be so accustomed to his schemes that we are able to diagnose our children's experiences as if we were well skilled doctors. The writer of Ecclesiastes reminds us that there is nothing new or different under the sun, that what has been, will be again; and what has been done will be repeated *(Ecclesiastes 1:9-10)* - if we do not do something to change it. When we sense that Satan is attacking our kids with a similar situation that we or someone in our family tree may have experienced at their age, this is not the time to laugh it off as a cute coincidence, or run coward in fear by hiding our heads in the sands hoping that the problem will go away.

When I was around 19 years old, I was rushed to the hospital by a family member because I was experiencing some pretty bad stomach pain. As the doctors spent nearly an hour taking test and trying to figure out the cause of my discomfort, my mother walked in the room and after two seconds of seeing me she said with confidence, "Girl, ain't nothing wrong with you. You pregnant in yo tubes!"

The medical term for this type of pregnancy is ectopic. Minutes later the doctor would come in and confirm my mother's accurate diagnosis. Although, I was in immense pain, I can still remember being so impressed with my Mom's precise verdict of my situation. Later, I would ask her how she knew that I was experiencing a tubal pregnancy. She told me it was because she had experienced the same thing around my age and all of my signs indicated that I was undergoing the same type of miscarriage. "Wow," I thought. "Just like that, experience can beat a Doctor at a diagnosis?"

Years later, when I became a Mom, I would use the same skill that I learned from my Mother on that day at the hospital to diagnose my daughter of the many things that she would face that I had gone through at her age. Because I had grown up without my father in the home, I knew when her attitude shifted and the cloud of depression lurked over her head due to missing the presence of her dad. When little boys began to play and act mean toward her, I was able to share with her that their cruelty was usually because they liked her and how to stand up for herself. I can name countless experiences that she went through that I was able to successfully maneuver her through because of that event at the hospital with my Mom. Because she was teachable and eager to do the right thing, this saved her a lot of undue turmoil and heartache during her teen years. This also helped her to develop a trust for me and I became her number one go to person when any type of problem came up in her life.

God wants to use this skill in the lives of all believers who have kids to help them to recognize and overcome Satan's tactics when it comes to keeping our children out of sexual sin. Was your great granddaddy, poppa a rolling stone? Has your little Jr. grown up and is living a lewd lifestyle, having babies with women he's not married to all over the state in which you live, without a job, or means to take care of them? Is your daughter in a promiscuous rebellious state, sneaking boys into her room like you did, and your mother did, and her mother did when you all were her age?

Fear not, that is not your child. The real culprit is satan trying to continue the curse through your family's lineage. You have authority over your past, present and your future through the Blood of Jesus. Plead the Blood of Jesus over your past, present, and future. Use the prayer for Parents at the end of this book to uproot any demonic seeds sown by you and/or your ancestors that may now be coming up against the child's life. It is your job as a spirit-filled born again believer of God to reverse that curse off of your children's lives through prayer with The Word of God.

When we recognize the enemy for who he is, we can finally, stop fighting with our children. This does not mean that we do not need to discipline our children, holding them accountable for their choices. It means we can quit dealing with symptoms and confront the source, satan with the Truth that is found in God's

Word. For we wrestle not against flesh and blood but against principalities, powers, and spirits of darkness in heavenly places (*Ephesians 6:12*). Once we have identified the true perpetrator, we are ready to help our children make wise choices through the process of relational parenting.

Relational Parenting

Relational parenting is a parenting style in which parents take information, situations, and circumstances of their pasts (good or bad) and relate these things to their children in the timing of God by the wisdom of God. This is done so that children will not repeat their parent's negative past in their futures. When we can identify and relate to our children's circumstances, this is the building block to a more intimate relationship with them.

Relational parenting makes parents:

- The coolest person in a kid's life.
- The go-to person when kids are having problems.
- The confidant that kids rely on because they are able to see that parents really do understand them.

When parents can relate to their children, kids are less apt to run to their friends or society to answer the questions about their sexual dilemmas. Please keep in mind that although Relational Parenting decreases the likelihood of our children making our mistakes, the choice to do right is still up to our children.

My maternal grandmother, Momma Layton is a master at relating to her children and grandchildren her history through the art of storytelling. Anytime we are around her she can be counted on to tell us a story or two about herself, during her younger years. She has passed this gift on to my mother, aunts, uncles, and to her grandchildren.

A reoccurring story that I heard from my grandmother, as a child was how she and my great aunts were liked by all the boys and some of the other girls didn't like it and sort of picked with them over it. The first time that I heard the account, I thought it was an innocent cute story that Momma Layton told to let us in on her childhood mishaps. As time passed my Mom began to tell me stories about how she and my aunts literally got into fist fights with girls over guys, and how ugly these altercations had gotten. I did not think to link my grandmother's innocent disputes, as seeds of my mother's fist fights, until I had manifestations in my own life of a fight with a woman over a man.

When Jai got older and began to deal with this type of petty behavior from young women who may have liked the same guy that she talked to, I did not dismiss it as some would, thinking it as a simple petty encounter that kids go through. I also did not use the incident to swell Jai's head up in thinking everyone around her is jealous of her. I saw it as a continued demonic attack on the women in our family that had to be stopped. I talked the situation over with God and took authority over it by informing Jai of what she was up against. In the meanwhile, Jai and I allowed God to give us some practical ways to stop this nuisance spirit in our family by causing Jai to take responsibility for her own actions, helping her to realize that she does not fight over boys, and building up her self-esteem so that she knows who she is in Christ. I do the same thing with sexual sin.

When I recognize that the devil is trying to influence Jai sexually, I relate to her by sharing with her that I experienced the same or similar situation, the negative and positive ways that I handled it and all possible outcomes so that she can choose life or the best result for her particular circumstance.

There is NOTHING that I don't discuss with Jai concerning my past. Not so that we can be best buddies or that I am trying to be cool and fit in with her but so that she will not repeat my past in her future. She knows how I lost my virginity at age 13 to a guy seven years my senior who after the act, laughed at me and told all my friends how stiff I was during the process. She knows of the shame that I felt and how devastating this was for me. She knows that I have regrets about this situation. I now know that this time should have been a time of pleasure and joy shared with my husband, as a first time experience on our wedding day, instead of a nightmare.

(Although I was sexually violated as a younger child, penetration would not happen until I lost my virginity at age thirteen).

She knows that most boys will tell her, "I love you," to get sex and that she's more prone as a woman to want to give sex, in order to feel loved. She knows how to take her emotions to God when she is feeling this way, and she knows how to pray in the time of sexual temptation. She knows about my daddy hurt and how I used sex to try and fill this void. She knows how the enemy doesn't invent any new tricks and that even though her father has always been very much involved in her life, because he was not in our home that the enemy will try and use his physical absence to attack her with these same feelings that I experienced. Everything that we have gone through is so that our kids won't have to.

Once we have related our similar situations to our children we must take it a step further by telling them how we handled it, and the favorable or less than favorable outcome. If the outcome was good and we were not saved remind them that it was God's Grace keeping you. If the outcome was not favorable, let them know where you failed. Did you know about God's Grace? Did you ignore the warning signs of your parents or other adults? How could you have handled it different according to The Word? Be sure to ask for their input on ideas or suggestions of better ways that you could have handle it.

Do role plays, write out quick scripts together, have fun, but relate. Then go back to their situation and help them draw every possible outcome they can (good or bad). When you're done, let

God's Word have the final say. What does God's Word say about it? How may their friends respond? What does God's Word say about being a man pleaser? This process helps our children to develop critical thinking skills and the ability to make Godly choices according to Deuteronomy 30:19.

Parents You Have Influence

As a little girl, I was so in love with my Mother (and I still am). I thought that she was the most beautiful woman in the world. Not just because of her outer beauty, but I was enamored by her inner strength. I thought she could do anything and I wanted nothing more than to please her. What captivated me most about my Mom was the skill and time she took to talk to me in a loving and caring fashion. She spoke to me about all of the dos and don'ts of life like an accomplished orator. I don't know how it happened but she had me convinced to do everything that she told me to do. Yes, I went through stages of rebellion like most kids do, but everything my Mom asked me to do, I did it.

She told me, "Pearl (my nickname), go to school and get your education. Get a good job. Buy a house, car, and have your own. Do not have to depend on men for anything." She was not bitter with men; her experiences had taught her that a woman should have something to bring to the relationship as well. She also constantly told me, "Don't have no babies." When I came of age I did just what she told me. I obtained my own. I got my education, a house, car, job, and I did not have any children (until age 21).

I had sex, used birth control, I even had abortions. I did everything I could to grant my Mother her request of not having any babies. Sometime after I became a Mother myself, I could not help but wonder how things would have been had my Mother told me, "Pearl, don't have sex."

Because of the influence that she had on me and the love that I had and still have for her, I can't help but think that I would have done what she said as I had in all of the other areas in my life. Be specific in relaying your sexual expectations for your kids. When you're having "*the talk*" with them, don't just tell them not to bring babies to your house, tell them not to have sex. Raise your expectation of them. Just because you didn't wait does not mean that they can't.

I realize this is uncomfortable to a lot of parents because some of us are not at peace with our own past. We have not given God our sexual past and we don't view it in the light of His Word which states, it is washed in the Blood *(1 John 1:7)*. In fact, some of you are reading this right now and are so overtaken with the thought of having to discuss your sexual past with your child that it almost makes you nauseous. My friend, you have to overcome this fear with the help of God, to save your kids from your sexual pitfalls.

Nothing is too hard for God. We have made sex bigger than God. Every knee must bow and every tongue must confess that

Jesus Christ is Lord, (*Ephesians 2:10);* and that includes sexual sin. Yes, it's true our kids are going to do what they want to do away from our presence, but we cannot leave their decisions to luck, chance, or fate. As parents we have got to do all that we can to ensure that their choice is an informed choice and not a blind choice.

Anytime that I hear of a young person fathering or mothering a child out of wedlock, one of the first questions that comes to my mind is, were they informed? Did they really know and understand the consequence of their choice? Had anyone sat down with them and not only *told* them but *showed* them how to live a celibate life? I wonder had anyone consistently and strategically related to them? Were they given and shown how to walk out the mission and vision of the Christian family to wait for marriage to have sex? Were they aware of their Christian legacy of celibacy or virginity until marriage? I am saddened to know that nine times out of ten, the answer is no. That this baby having a baby has made a blind uninformed decision that will alter the face of his or her future forever. Don't allow your family to become a statistic. Incorporate the legacy of celibacy concept into your family.

God favors you! Getting pregnant or getting someone pregnant before marriage is devastating not only to the unwed couple but the families of either the boy or the girl. I don't care how cute a baby is or how much we love them; a teen pregnancy alters the entire life of the teens and their parents. Their God-ordained destiny is prolonged or even aborted if they never recover from their sexual choice. This is all because they decided to add a baby into the equation. A baby changes everything!

It is my belief that you can't miss what you've never had. I encourage teens and adults who have never had sex, not to have sex until you are married to the man or woman that God has designed for you. Steer clear of sexual sin. If you are like me when I was a teen and no one has ever told you not to have sex, I want to take the time to tell you, Don't do it! DO NOT HAVE SEX UNTIL YOU ARE MARRIED! MARRY A MAN OR WOMAN OF GOD that you have spent time getting to know and who knows you. MARRY AS A VIRGIN TO A VIRGIN!

As a side note, I would like to stress to virgins not to toy around or dabble in sex. I cannot stress it enough that not having sex before marriage, is about honoring God. Honoring God sexually is not just about not entering a penis into a vagina, or breaking a hymen. I know that we have already talked about the major types of sex in Chapter Three: "The Freaky Five," but I want to emphasize that sex is the involvement of any of one's members in sexual activity. Honoring God sexually means to keep one's members away from sexual activity. One's members include the:

- Mind
- Mouth
- Will
- Emotions
- Hands
- Penis
- Vagina
- Anus
- Or any other part of a person's being not mentioned.

Be sure to follow the 7-Secrets of Celibacy:

1. **Get Saved, For Real:** Get to know God by accepting Him into your heart as your personal Lord and Savior.
2. **Develop Discipline:** Become a doer of The Word by practicing the discipline needed to stay in a committed relationship with God.
3. **Know Your Hot Spots**: Because you're not sexually active you will need to get a trusted mentor who will navigate you through locating your hot spots. Don't

allow one person of the opposite sex to take up all of your time, befriend multiple people of God who interest you.

4. **Passionately Pursue Purpose:** Finish college, start a business, save money, travel around the world, mentor smaller children who look up to you.

5. **Have Fun But Don't Give 'em None:** While dating have as much fun as you possible can while remaining sexually pure.

6. **Give God "That" Part of Your Heart:** Make God's priority, your priority. Be determined to put a smile on God's face by making what is important to God important to you. Win souls into the Kingdom of God. Spend an adequate amount of your time, talent and treasure in building Kingdom projects.

7. **Don't Quit!:** Don't grow weary in well doing for in due season you will date and marry the person God has for you (if that is your heart's desire).

If you want to marry someone exciting, become that someone that you would like to marry. Get around positive people who will motivate and encourage you towards your God given purpose. God always does above and beyond what we could ask or think. Don't allow peer pressure and societal norms to make you think that you are missing out on something by making the choice not to have sex. Know that love is not sex, and sex is not love. Do not be fooled into thinking that you have to have sex to be cool or fit in. You are accepted by God *(Ephesians 1:6)*.

Ask God to let His acceptance of you to be enough. You won't do everything perfect but there are some mistakes that you cannot afford to make. Sexual sin is one of those mistakes.

When my daughter was a teen, I compared her life to mine when I was her age. It is hard to believe how blessed she is in comparison to me at her age. She had no needs, she maintained an excellent work ethic, and God was always using someone to bless her life. While her father and I were not together as she grew up, she had both parents in her life. Her blessings were different from mine as a teenager. As I began to ask God why she was so blessed, He began to minister to my spirit that Jai had been so blessed because she was pure in heart. Matthew 5:8 reads, "Blessed are the pure in heart for they shall see God."

He continued to show me that the meaning of this passage as it pertained to Jai's life was that being pure in heart did not mean being perfect in heart. It simply meant a heart that is right toward God. And because she had a pure heart she experienced the blessing of God and had the privilege of seeing God manifest Himself to her, everyday of her life! I was floored by this explanation of scripture. He continued to speak to my spirit that this does not mean that she would not go through things or have problems but she would see God bring her through victoriously, in every obstacle she faced.

She had not only been pure toward God, her family, and others, as a teen, she was also pure sexually and because she honored God in her body, he honored her by blessing her. She left for college to study to become a Doctor. She has written and published a children's book entitled, "A Day on Emma Leigh's Farm © 2010. She has been on cruises and seen some parts of the world that some people twice her age will never see. This is all because she had made the choice to be pure in heart.

I am not dumb enough to think that Jai does not make her own choices about her body, but they will not be blind choices. She has been informed. God wants to do the same for you. Determine to live a life free from sexual sin and watch God do things in your life that you could have only dreamed of!

3

Prayers
For Freedom
Over Sexual Sin

Father, in the name of Jesus I thank You that because I have made the decision to keep myself pure, I am blessed and highly favored by You and man. Father, I ask that You give me the wisdom needed to steer clear of sexual sin, until You send me the mate that You have designed specifically for me. I ask that You help me to guard my heart with all diligence for out of it flows the issues of my life. I thank You Father that because bad company corrupts good morals, I am not enticed to hang out with or date bad company.

I thank You that just like Joseph took the way of escape from Potiphar's wife; I too flee sexual immorality, in Jesus' name. I thank You that because I make the choice to be pure in heart, I see You move in my life, all the days of my life. I thank You that I am not anxious to be in a relationship, to have sex or for anything else. I pray about everything and I thank You for the answer. Father, In the Name of Jesus, I thank You that I am teachable. I am not wise in my own eyes or prudent in my own sight. I don't know everything. I seek and obey sound instruction. I am insightful because I can accurately discern right from wrong. I do not use the excuse that I am young as the opportunity to make misinformed mistakes.

I realize that I am accountable for what I do to You, my parents, family and friends. Thank You that because I have a passionate pursuit of purpose I am focused on my destiny in You. I don't judge others and I won't be judged by others. I am humble, repentant, yet bold in You to walk uprightly when those around me chose to go the other way.

Father, I thank You that I am not moved by the opinions and persecution of man for I am a God pleaser and not a man pleaser. Therefore, I rejoice when I am persecuted for Your names sake because great is my reward on this earth. Thank You that because I do not grow weary in well doing in due season I will reap because I won't faint. Thank You Daddy that I have Godly mentors, friends, and family who encourages me to stay on the straight and narrow path of virginity. I do not yield to the seemingly popular ways of the world and the lust of the flesh. When I am tempted, I simply say, "Jesus is Lord over my entire life, including my flesh and He will not put anything on me that I cannot bear." Thank You Father, that because I choose to wait on You to have sex in the marriage covenant, I will not be ashamed or confused in Jesus' name, Amen.

Prayer for Parents

Father in the name of Jesus, I thank You that my child (name) will marry as a virgin to a virgin a man or woman of God who shares the same beliefs and values that are outlined in Your Word. Thank You Father that You said that if I trained my child (name) up in the way that they should go that when they are old, they will not depart from You and Your way of doing things.

Father I speak wisdom and maturity over my child (name) right now in the name of Jesus. I thank You that my child (name) is a doer of The Word and not a hearer only, that he/she is teachable and eager to do things Your way and not the worlds way and that includes saving their bodies for sex until they are married.

Father God I ask that You help me as his/her parent to be an example of what it means to be sexually pure. I repent for all of the ways that I may have sinned sexually rather in thought, Word or deed. I uproot any ungodly seed of fornication, lust, and adultery that I have sown by my own actions that may try to attach itself to the life of my children, in the name of Jesus. I thank You that new seeds of purity, holiness, and faithfulness is planted, watered, rooted, and made manifest in my life and the lives of my children. I give You all praise honor and glory that the curse of sexual immorality has been broken off of my blood line right now in Jesus' name, Amen.

Prayer for Non-Virgins

Father in the name of Jesus, I repent for giving myself to sexual sin. I thank You that my body is the temple of the Holy Ghost and I choose to flee sexual immorality. I thank You Father that there is now therefore no condemnation to those who are in Christ Jesus, who walk not after the flesh but after the Spirit. Thank You Daddy that from this day forward I choose to walk after the Spirit and not according to my flesh. I thank You that because I have authority over snakes and scorpions, I also have authority over the lust of my flesh and its appetites.

Father, thank You that I take the time to uproot the ungodly seeds of fornication, lust, and adultery from my life that may have been planted years ago by my ancestors; and now have attached themselves to my life. In the name of Jesus, I plant new seeds of purity, holiness and faithfulness. Thank You that because I am now pure in heart I can see You manifested in my life every day of my life; all the days of my life. Thank You that I have the stamina to wait on Your best in the area of a mate because I don't grow weary in well doing. Thank You that I am content during this time of singleness.

Thank You Father for doing exceedingly abundantly above all that I could ask think or imagine because I choose to honor You with my body and therefore You honor me with Your best for my life. Thank You that better is a bread crumb shared in love than prime rib served in hate. I'd rather be single and happy than married or connected to the wrong person and miserable. I thank You that this statement is not to let you off the hook in manifesting my mate. It simply confirms that I will not settle for just anything or anybody, when I am entitled to Your best in every area of my life. I thank You that I am never really alone because You said You would never leave or forsake me.

Thank You that I don't make excuses for You when I don't see Your promises manifest. Instead I eagerly wait with excitement and anticipation for Your best in the form of a mate; in Jesus' name I pray, Amen.

Father at times I feel as if I were born gay because I just am not attracted to the opposite sex and I am unsure why. There are also times that I am convinced that I like both men and women and I don't see the harm in having the best of both worlds. I ask that You return the natural desire for the opposite sex to my heart. Because You are not the Author of confusion but of peace, I thank You for Your best in the area of my identity and a mate.

God I ask that You uproot the spirit of homosexuality out of my life. I ask that You plant, water, root and make manifest the proper mannerism connected with the sex that You have made me. Because You created me as a man (if you were born male) with a penis, I act, think, dream, dress, walk, marry, perform sexually and talk like a man. Because You have created me as a woman (if you were born female) with a vagina, I act, think, dream, dress, walk, marry, perform sexually and talk like a woman. God You said that You would reveal all things to me. Please show me why I have rejected who You have created me to be as all male, or all female.

Your Word says that I am accepted of the beloved and that You love me so much that You gave Your only son for me. God, I thank You that You are not mad at me. You Love me and You don't reject me. Instead, like all other sin, You reject the sin of homosexuality in my life. Because You desire truth in the inward part, You know all things, and nothing is hidden from You, I come clean with the sin of homosexuality. I won't hide it from You, myself, or others. As You reveal to me the root cause of homosexuality in my life help me not to run from You but to run to You, my one and only help.

God I can't be healed without You. I apologize that I have made homosexual sin bigger than You thinking that I can't overcome it, when there is nothing bigger than You. I plead the Blood of Jesus over my sexual past, present and future. Because, nothing can penetrate the Blood of Jesus, I thank You for the victory over homosexuality. As I walk in my victory over the sin of homosexuality, I thank You for the boldness to help others to freedom with the same grace, mercy and love that You have afforded me, in Jesus' name I pray, Amen.

Prayer for Freedom over Masturbation, Oral Sex, Sodomy & Pornography

Father in the name of Jesus, I thank You that You are my God. I apologize for the self-indulgent sin of masturbation, oral sex sodomy, and/or pornography. God my only desire is to please You and if pleasing You means the discontinuance of what I consider as fun sex, what is socially acceptable sex, and/or what feels good to my lower nature sex, please give me a genuine desire to stop. Father, honestly I'm not sure if I believe that either masturbation, oral sex, sodomy, and/or pornography is considered sin, so I ask that You show me at my level of comprehension that it is wrong. When You show me, Father give me the strength to do things Your way sexually.

217

Father, the last thing I want to do is knowingly or unknowingly hurt You so I ask for Your help in transforming me as I renew my mind about what it takes to fulfill my sexual appetite. God, I ask that You uproot the seed sown by any one in my family's history or myself that would feed the sin of masturbation, oral sex, sodomy, and/or pornography. I curse every perverted word spoken over me that would feed the desire for me to practice the sexual sin of masturbation, oral sex, sodomy, and/or pornography. I thank You that new seeds of holiness is planted, watered, rooted and made manifest in my life.

Your Word says that the marriage bed is undefiled, but whoremongers and adulterers would be judged. God I ask that You would create in me a clean heart and renew a right spirit within me. When I am tempted to sin sexually please cause me to enter into pure worship where I am reminded that You are my first love and where the fragments of my soul can be made whole. Daddy God, I ask that You heal every emotional wound with the balm of Gilead. I plead the Blood of Jesus over every dark place in my being that would draw me back to sexual sin which includes masturbation, oral sex, sodomy, and/or masturbation. Thank You that every dark place is now made light by the power of Your Word.

Father, You are more than enough and I don't need illicit sex to be fulfilled. Thank You for my new found freedom in You. Thank You that You will not only save me but You will keep me. Therefore, I do not have to fear returning to the error of my old sexual ways and habits. Thank You for Your best in the area of a mate and that my marriage will be a living testament of Your Goodness and love in Jesus name, Amen.

4

Final
Thoughts

There, I said it! I can't tell you the spiritual, emotional, financial, and physical turmoil that I have endured to process this book in my head and to get it on paper wondering if the world would feel I was being too harsh. Would the church think I am qualified? Is the topic of celibacy in the church as relevant as I portray it? Will my daughter be put under a microscope for my transparency in sharing my sexual experiences? Would my colleagues think that I am a freak? What would my future husband think? Am I committing marital suicide before I even get up the isle? Will the man of my dreams have the ability to look pass my past to see who God has made me to be now?

While talking to a confidant about the direction that this book was taking, I was asked,

"Have you always been this transparent when it comes to talking about your life?"

My response,

"Yes, with myself."

I have always been true and honest with me but due to the fear of rejection I have always transformed into a relational chameleon, in an attempt to make others feel comfortable."

I have done this so much that over time, I have learned how not to be me around people. By nature, I am a peace maker. I have discovered, over the years, that I had become more comfortable with making peace with everyone else except myself.

As much as I know that this book will be a blessing to all those who read it, it has been more therapeutic for me in that I am finally at peace with myself. I am comfortable with knowing who I was before Christ. I am comfortable with who I am now in Christ, and excited about where I am going with Christ. This book has allowed me to display all three of these areas and it is the most freeing feeling in the world.

It is my prayer that you, my reader, will experience an even greater freedom as you allow God to peel back the layers of pretense that comes along with living in sexual sin. My biggest prayer is that everyone who reads this book would feel the love, mercy, and grace of God as you face sexual sin, head on through the power of God. Thank you for allowing me to share my journey to sexual purity. Remember that God loves you to life! Be Blessed!

Margaret

NOTES

NOTES

Frierson, M. G. (Performer). (2013). Authentic Living: Life Accroding to God's Plan. Saginaw, Michigan, United States of America.

Cooper, D. L., & Haynie, B. (n.d.). Retrieved March 29, 2014, from Biblical Research Studies Group: http://biblicalresearch.info/index.html

Frierson, G. (Composer). (2014). A Kingdom Woman: Kingdom Identity and Purpose. Saginaw, Michigan, United States of America.

Frierson, D. G. (Performer). (2000). Living In The Empowerment Zone. Saginaw, MI, United States of America.

Merriam-Webster. (2014, August). Retrieved January 1, 2014, from Merriam-Webster Web site: www.Merriam-Webster.com/dictionary/sodomy

Shakespeare, P. (2001). *Hamlet.* New York: Penguin Group.

Slick, M. (2013, September). *CARM: Christian Apologetics & Research Ministry*. Retrieved September 16,

2013, from CARM: http://carm.org/what-is-the-purpose-of-marriage

Frierson, D. R. (Performer). (2001). Stages of Relationships. Saginaw, Michigan.

The Lockman Foundation. (1981, 1988). *Bible Hub: NAS Exhaustive Concordance of The Bible.* Retrieved March 29, 2014, from Bible Hub: www.http//biblehub.com/hebrew/1692.htm

Trimm, C. (2011, September 1). *Dr. Cindy Trimm with TD Jakes on TBN - Sep 01, 2011 Interview & Testimony.* Retrieved March 29, 2014, from www.youtube.com/watch?v=bVu3XzqCf_M

BE ON THE LOOK OUT FOR FUTURE RELEASES

by Margaret S. Layton
& Black Pearl Publishing, LLC

Visit Margaret's Blog or Book Margaret to host
your next event at:

WWW.MargaretSLayton.com

e-mail Margaret at:

MargaretLayton@sbcglobal.net